A HIGHER

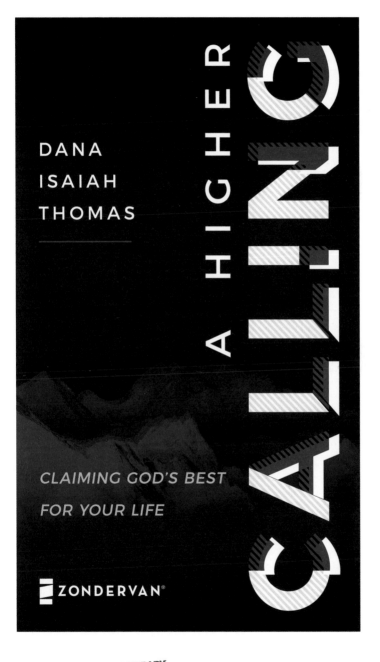

DANA
ISAIAH
THOMAS

A HIGHER CALLING

CLAIMING GOD'S BEST
FOR YOUR LIFE

ZONDERVAN®

ZONDERVAN

A Higher Calling
Copyright © 2018 by Dana Isaiah Thomas

This title is also available as a Zondervan ebook.

Requests for information should be addressed to:
Zondervan, *3900 Sparks Dr. SE, Grand Rapids, Michigan 49546*

ISBN 978-0-310-76653-7 (print)

ISBN 978-0-310-76649-0 (ebook)

Art direction: DogEared Design / Kirk DouPonce
Interior design: Denise Froehlich

Printed in China

18 19 20 21 22 / DSC / 10 9 8 7 6 5 4 3 2 1

Shortly after finding out that A Higher Calling *was actually going to happen, I met my friend Rasual Butler. He played at the highest level of basketball and was an overall great man. He opened up to me right away as we watched our significant others sing and laugh together. The very next day, I sent him one of these devotions and told him about the book. He was so excited, he told me he couldn't wait to buy a copy and send it to his buddies in the NBA and Philly. It brought me so much joy to hear his excitement. Just as the editing process wrapped up, Rasual and his beautiful wife, Leah, died in a car accident. Although I hadn't known Rasual for long, we had a profound impact on each other's lives. We had a bond that no one could break, and that bond was Jesus. I dedicate this book to Rasual Butler, a great friend and an even better man. May your legacy live on forever.*

Contents

Foreword

Being in the entertainment industry, the illusion of comfort and success is everywhere. You see chiseled bodies but not the pain of working out. We see riches without the struggle of having to work and sacrifice. We see beaches, fun, adventure, entertainment, and success, but not the pain and suffering that may have been endured to get it. Most of us want those things because we think they bring us comfort.

Here's a reality check: God doesn't call us to comfort. God calls us to his kingdom.

To be successful in life, we have to re-orient our idea of success. Success is not what we do compared to others, but what we do compared to what we were created for.

Our comfort has little to do with this kind of success.

God is a perfect ruler with a perfect agenda. You and me, however, are imperfect. Still, he's gracious enough to give us the opportunity to be ambassadors of his kingdom. Our purpose is greater than self-satisfaction; it's being a part of the Creator's plans.

Knowing this should inspire us to stop working out of grit grind and start depending on God's powers.

I've worked with a lot of athletes who have seen time and time again that our own human willpower and strength can fail us. Injuries can sideline a player's whole career.

God's strength, in comparison, is eternal. It never fades, and is consistent and reliable.

Samson was the strongest man of his day, Solomon the wisest, and David had a sincere passion for God, yet they all failed.

Failure shows us our imperfections and need to grow. How can you grow? By being dependent on God, his word, and his ways.

There will be plenty of work on your part. No one is saying that simply reading and praying is all you need to do to become successful. But the work and the worship are all combined. As a matter of fact, we should work out of a heart to worship God.

Again, success is not how much you've done compared to others but how much you've done compared to what you were created to do.

Remember, your life is not your own—you are a living sacrifice. You are here to show the world what God can do with an imperfect person like yourself. Whether that's in business, fashion, entertainment, sports, or whatever.

We have to remember God is in control, not our consultant.

You're always one step away from change, and reading this book is taking that step.
God bless,
Lecrae

A Special Note from Dana's Dad

Few things in life are more meaningful than passing the baton of faith. The joy of seeing your child take it and then pass it along to others is one of those joys, in my opinion. Watching my son grow through the stages of life, sharing what he has learned with others, is rewarding to me as a parent. Life has a way of teaching us many lessons, and sometimes those lessons are clothed in painful experiences. Whether it is the consequences of an unwise decision or the reality of an unanticipated injury, each of these experiences has something to teach us. Sometimes it takes a while to learn or understand, but the value is in the learning experience. Dana understands the value of reflection and the wisdom of learning from others to help him grow from these experiences.

The thoughts shared in this devotional come from a life that is still being forged. Dana's life experiences have uniquely shaped him to encourage others. Born into a home with parents in vocational ministry, he had to navigate all the expectations and attention placed on a PK (pastor's kid). The pressure of being a good athlete and student only magnified those expectations as he learned to own and walk out the faith he professed. It was both the successes and the failures that equipped him to share from experience. So many lose sight of the value of failure. Yet the scriptures are filled with people who failed that God still used for his glory. It is my prayer that God will use this devotional to encourage others who are walking through life. I am sure you will be encouraged as you read these devotions written from an athlete's perspective.

Introduction

I've experienced a lot over the past twenty-something years. You know, first loves, the heartache that comes with breaking up, illness and injury, loneliness, rejection, and the consequences of bad decisions. The challenges and trials we go through in life can seem like tidal waves threatening to drown us. It's not something I talk about often, but at the age of eighteen I even tried to take my own life. God clearly had a different plan, because after that dark night, I woke up, and I am here today as a testament to his amazing grace.

I never thought I would have the courage to write because I never thought, before now, I had anything to say. But God has changed my life so much that I want to encourage you to let him change you too. You see, throughout all the chaos in my life—a career-changing injury, a cancer diagnosis, depression, suicide—there was one thing that remained consistent. And that one thing was God's presence.

My life verse is 2 Corinthians 12:9 (NLT): "'My grace is all you need. My power works best in weakness.' So now I am glad to boast about my weaknesses, so that the power of Christ can work through me." It's a great reminder that God can use anyone despite their mess. This verse strengthens me when doubt surrounds me. This verse has challenged me to remain humble in all situations. And this verse has encouraged me to keep my eyes on Jesus, because he is the one who holds my life together.

A Higher Calling was birthed out of the mess God walked me through. It offers a devotion for each day of the month with accompanying Scriptures to challenge and encourage you. If you aren't able to read a devotion every day, set yourself a six- or twelve-month plan and read two or three devotions a week. Don't be afraid to journal, underline, and highlight whenever something stands out. I pray that this book pushes you to seek Christ no matter what circumstances you encounter. Remember what James says in James 1:2–4 (NLT): "Dear brothers and sisters, when troubles of any kind come your way, consider it an opportunity for great joy. For you know that when your faith is tested, your endurance has a chance to grow. So let it grow, for when your endurance is fully developed, you will be perfect and complete, needing nothing." Know that trials of various kinds will come throughout your life, and no matter what the trial is, God will always be there to walk with you through it all. He is a faithful God who never leaves us. We can always count on him!

1

All Faith, No Fear

Now faith is confidence in what we
hope for and assurance about what
we do not see.

HEBREWS 11:1

I was hundreds of miles away from home as a freshmen student at the Air Force Academy Preparatory School in Colorado Springs. I was homesick and couldn't wait to see my family at Christmas break. Little did I know that would be the start of the most difficult period I have faced in my life.

When Christmas break finally arrived a few weeks later, I headed home. But I wasn't greeted with the happy welcome I had envisioned. My parents announced that my dad would be having surgery to remove a goiter the following day. This came as a surprise because my dad looked strong and healthy, just as he had always appeared.

I sat with my two siblings and my mom in the

hospital while we waited for the doctors to finish the surgery. But before we were allowed to see him, there was another nasty surprise. We learned that the doctors had discovered two different types of thyroid cancer. The treatment plan was intense—my dad would need his thyroid removed and then undergo radiation treatment. His body would never be the same again.

My dad was my real-life hero. I was devastated! I sat in silence, gripped by fear, anger, and confusion. I was afraid the treatments would fail and that I would lose my dad. The cancer seemed so sudden, so random. I knew my dad didn't deserve this terrible twist of fate, so how could this be happening?

We were finally allowed to see Dad in the recovery room. And just as quickly as fear took hold of me in the waiting room, once I was with my dad, I felt the physical presence and peace of God settle over me. There sat my dad, an enormous smile on his face despite the awful news he had learned. And what's more, he was telling the hospital staff about his faith—that he believed in a God who was far bigger than cancer, and that he was not afraid. On one of the worst days of my dad's life, he chose not to give in to fear. Instead, he remembered the love of God and shared it with those around him. In that moment, Dad taught me how to trust that no matter what I faced, God was bigger.

Jeremiah 32:17 says, "Ah, Sovereign LORD, you have made the heavens and the earth by your great power and outstretched arm. Nothing is too hard for you." Whatever you're up against today, no matter how big the mountain is in front of you, keep your eyes on our powerful God.

My dad knew that cancer *could* take his life. But even with that knowledge, he chose to not be anxious about it and instead trusted that however things turned out, God was in control. God is bigger than any of our problems. And like my dad telling the nurses about Jesus, God can use our problems to bring about good things.

As we drove home from the hospital, I thought about the fact that my dad, my hero and my role model, had cancer . . . but cancer didn't have him. I was still scared—I cried as my sister held my hand—but I was learning to trust God more than I trusted my fear. This was a major turning point in my walk with God because I realized that, as followers of Christ, we are called to be people of faith, not people of fear.

If you are not sure whether your faith is strong enough to trust God more than fear, more than the problems you're facing, don't worry. In my experience, faith doesn't feel like 100 percent confidence that everything will be perfect in the end. If that were the case, it wouldn't be faith; it would be fact. But faith is being sure that, even though we don't know how things will end, we can trust God will work it out for good. Faith is being sure that God hears your prayers, even if you don't see the answers yet. Faith is knowing that anxiety and fear don't control you. Faith is being sure that, even on your worst days, God is good.

Do you have the faith to trust Christ through every

Faith is being sure that, even though we don't know how things will end, we can trust God will work it out for good.

situation? If you're still not sure, don't give up. In Mark 9:24, we find a father who is struggling to believe that Jesus can and will heal his son. He wants to believe, but he feels his faith shaking. He begs Jesus, "Help me overcome my unbelief!" Sometimes we have to pray this prayer—asking Jesus to help us as we try to place all our faith and trust in him. God will help you. Sometimes he encourages us through the words of the Bible, or through a conversation with a friend or family member. Other times, he will calm your anxiety, giving you peace and hope.

I am pleased to say that now, my dad is cancer-free and healthy. All glory be to God! And as for me, that was just the start of my journey to discovering my higher calling.

REFLECT

Reflect on that truth that God, who knows all things, is never surprised at what happens in our lives. Even if we're overwhelmed by our circumstances, he isn't. In the Psalms, we read that God holds all creation in the palm of his hand, and that includes you. As you journal and pray today, open your heart to God and share with him all your concerns and fears. And thank him for his constant love and faithfulness. Ask him to help you grow in your faith and trust in his good plans.

2

A Gracious God

In him we have redemption through
his blood, the forgiveness of sins, in
accordance with the riches of God's
grace that he lavished on us.

EPHESIANS 1:7–8

Nothing we do will prevent us from receiving God's grace and forgiveness. Maybe this sounds too good to be true. Some people spend their whole lives thinking God is angry at them for something they did, or that God is holding a grudge against a group of people. But the greatest sin is still not as strong as God's love. In fact, many men and women of the Bible did terrible things, but God forgave them and still used their lives in amazing ways.

In the book of Acts, which takes place shortly after Jesus died and came back to life again, we read about a passionate Jew named Saul. Saul traveled all around the Middle East persecuting the followers of Jesus. He was a member of a group who did not believe Jesus was the Son of God, and they felt the need to protect their faith from those who did.

Saul hunted groups of Christians, dragging them to court and condemning them to death. By doing this, he thought he was helping God. People lost their jobs and belongings, were publicly humiliated, and were thrown out of their communities, imprisoned, and killed because of Saul's actions. Then one day, Jesus appeared to Saul and said, "Why do you persecute me?" Saul was blinded from the light of Jesus' appearance until God sent a believer to heal Saul's eyes and teach him the truth about who Jesus is.

This moment drastically changed Saul's life. From then on, Saul became known as Paul and traveled the world, teaching hundreds of thousands of people— including leaders, rulers, and emperors—about Jesus. See what Paul says about his story in 1 Timothy 1:12–14: "I thank Christ Jesus our Lord, who has given me strength, that he considered me trustworthy, appointing me to his service. Even though I was once a blasphemer and a persecutor and a violent man, I was shown mercy because I acted in ignorance and unbelief. The grace of our Lord was poured out on me abundantly, along with the faith and love that are in Christ Jesus." Paul went from persecuting the church with everything he had to giving his whole life to teaching others about Christ. What a transformation.

Many years before Paul lived, there was a man named David. David was Israel's greatest king, handpicked by God when he was just a boy. But still—after he had been following God for many years, knew how to listen and follow God's voice, and had seen God do amazing things—he messed up big time. David saw a woman and wanted her to be his wife, but she was already married to one of his soldiers. So David gave special instructions to his commander, and sent the solider to the battle's front line to die. The plan worked and David married the woman. Then God sent a prophet to David and showed him how wrong his actions were. Although David prayed and admitted his sin to God, he still had to live through the consequences of his sin. But God reminded David of his unconditional love by forgiving him and allowing him to remain king despite the murder he committed. And David continued to follow God and did many more good things for Israel.

In the book of Joshua, we meet Rahab, a woman who lived in the evil city of Jericho. At that time, the Israelites were conquering the land around Jericho, so they sent spies to scope out the area. As a citizen of Jericho, Rahab would have worshiped idols her whole life, praying and giving sacrifices to these false gods. And Rahab was a prostitute. But Rahab helped and protected the Israelite spies by hiding them from the king of Jericho in her house. She kept them safe, showed them how to escape the city, and then asked them to let her join God's people. Rahab stopped her work as a prostitute, gave up her religion to false idols, adopted a completely different culture, and moved away from her old home. It must have been hard and unnerving for her, but over time, she made Israel her new home. Rahab married and had a son and became the great-great-grandmother of King

David. Guess whose family line Jesus was born into? Yes—Rahab's.

God can and will change your life if you let him. If you have lived your whole life making bad choices and chasing after things instead of

God can and will change your life if you let him.

God, like Rahab, God wants to forgive you and give you a new life. If he can forgive and have grace on murderers like Paul and David, he can do the same for you.

We were born into a sinful world. We all sin—the preachers you see in the pulpit on Sunday, the evangelist who speaks around the world, and even the people you call mentors. But because God is gracious, he forgives sin when we admit our wrongs and try to live better. No sin is

Christ Jesus came into the world to save sinners.

so bad that it can't be wiped clean by his forgiveness. Paul, who knew firsthand how life-changing it is to be forgiven, says, "Christ Jesus came into the world to save sinners—of whom I am the worst. But for that very reason I was shown mercy so that in me, the worst of sinners, Christ Jesus might display his immense patience as an example for those who would believe in him and receive eternal life" (1 Timothy 1:15–16).

God, the great judge of all the earth, wants to forgive you and make you a new person. You only have to ask and Jesus will erase all your sin and all your guilt. Will you be perfect after? No, but there is nothing that can separate you from the forgiveness and love of God.

WRITE

Think about the sins you've done, big and small, recent and from a long time ago. In your journal, tell God you are sorry for your sins and ask him to forgive you. You can trust that God hears you and that you are forgiven. Jesus Christ came to earth and died for this very thing!

If you want to live in God's complete forgiveness and unconditional love for the rest of your life, then you may be ready to become a Christian. How do you do this? The only thing you have to do is pray. Admit to God that you are a sinner and that you need his forgiveness. Say you believe that Jesus Christ, the Son of God, came and died for your sins and was risen from the dead. Ask him to be Lord of your heart and life.

If you just prayed this prayer, welcome to God's family! I encourage you to tell someone else—a family member, friend, youth pastor, or teacher—so that they can come alongside you and help you grow as you learn how to be a Christ follower. Remember: nothing can separate you from Jesus' love. You are forgiven and free.

3

The Struggle

Then Jesus was led by the Spirit into the wilderness to be tempted by the devil. After fasting forty days and forty nights, he was hungry. The tempter came to him and said, "If you are the Son of God, tell these stones to become bread." Jesus answered, "It is written: 'Man shall not live on bread alone, but on every word that comes from the mouth of God.'"

MATTHEW 4:1–4

Have you ever decided to make a change for the better, and discovered that things got really hard, really fast? The very moment we make the decision to, say, exercise more, study harder, or be a kinder person, we mess up. We get sidetracked and default to old habits, or something riles us up and we lash out at a family member. We promise ourselves we're going to practice harder, but the next practice session goes terribly. Anytime we decide to make a change for the better, there's a good chance we will get pushback from the world and even from ourselves.

This makes us wonder if change is worth the effort and frustration. If we know things will only get harder before they get better, should we even try?

Frederick Douglass said, "If there is no struggle, there is no progress." Change costs us something—whether it's the time we would have spent online instead of studying or the effort to show kindness to a difficult person. Each of those sacrifices—those growing pains—means we're making progress toward becoming a better version of ourselves.

> "If there is no struggle, there is no progress."

Just as Jesus was preparing to go into full-time ministry, Matthew 4 tells us how he was led into the wilderness to fast and pray for forty days and forty nights. After this period of fasting, the devil came and tempted him in three different ways.

First, Satan attacked Jesus' identity as the Son of God. He taunted Jesus, saying that if Jesus was really the Son of God, he should turn stones into bread. He mocked Jesus' fast—something Jesus chose to do as an act of obedience to the Father. Second, Satan attacked Jesus' relationship with the Father. He told Jesus to challenge the Father's love and power by forcing angels to rescue him from death. Jesus, instead, chose faith—to not test God. Third, Satan attacked Jesus' mission. Jesus knew his mission would ultimately lead him to give up his life. But Satan offered him a shortcut. Instead of a path of sacrifice and love, Satan offered a path of ease and pride. But that was not the calling God had given Jesus.

Through all three temptations, Jesus did not waiver. He stood firm. This all happened just before Jesus' ministry went public. Was it coincidence that Satan picked this important time to launch a three-pronged attack? I don't think so. Just as Jesus was entering into obedience to God in a big way, he was faced with resistance.

Here's the kicker to the whole story: the Holy Spirit led Jesus into the wilderness for this trial. Why would God want Jesus to walk through the wilderness and face temptation? Don't misunderstand me, the Bible tells us God never tempts us. But sometimes he puts us in situations where we can grow, learn to trust his plan, and lean on his protection.

On the other hand, when Satan sees us taking our relationship with Christ to the next level, he will resist us. He even uses our own weaknesses against us, stirring up our doubts and fears and worries until we're paralyzed. He tries to make us stumble and fall so we get off track.

> When Satan sees us taking our relationship with Christ to the next level, he will resist us.

When you feel like you're wandering in the wilderness and being tempted by the devil, follow Jesus' example. Let nothing faze you, and remember to use the Word of God against any attacks. That's right—for every negative emotion you feel, for every drop of fear, there is a verse in the Bible that can encourage you and lift you up. God has left us Scripture to feel his comfort and his strength in hard times. James 1:2–4 says, "Consider it pure joy, my brothers and sisters, whenever you face trials of many kinds, because you know that the testing of your faith produces perseverance. Let perseverance finish its work so that you may be mature and complete, not lacking anything." I'm not saying that God desires for you to go through the trial you are experiencing right now. I don't think God ever wills for evil or terrible things to happen. But God can use all things to work together for your own spiritual growth so that you are a whole person, not lacking anything.

Know that when resistance seems more and more difficult, Jesus is always with you. He knows what it means to be pressed on every side and attacked. He also knows what it's like to live a loving, faithful life—he is the original role model! The devil hates to see us doing good for God; he hates our attempts at growing more into the person God has called us to be. But we can rise above his attacks. If you fall, get back up. If you stumble, keep walking.

Romans 5:3–5 tells us that our struggles create perseverance in us, which then strengthens our character. If there is no struggle, there is no progress. It might seem like your work isn't paying off yet. But as you keep pushing through the resistance—keep working, keep hustling—you will grow strong and resilient.

WRITE

In the same way that Jesus' mission was tested in the desert, we regularly experience struggles in our lives. Are you feeling push-back in your identity, your relationships, your life's calling? One way to learn how your faith is being challenged is to consider what kinds of faith questions keep circling in your mind, and what emotions you feel when you think about God. For example, if you keep wondering whether God really loves you or not, or if you feel nervous when you pray, then maybe you're feeling tested in your identity as a child of God.

Once you identify the area where you're facing resistance, you can start to grow. As you journal today, remind yourself of the truths you know already. In the example above, you can remind yourself that Jesus loves you so much, he died just so that he can be with you. Then write honestly about the struggle you're facing and ask God to help you grow through it.

4

Fractured Lives

Do not love this world nor the things
it offers you, for when you love the
world, you do not have the love of
the Father in you.

1 JOHN 2:15 (NLT)

The other day, one of my little brothers sent me a J. Cole song that talked about how people today relate more to modern songs and books than to the words in the Bible. It's easier for us to listen to a commercial than seek out the truth in a verse. It's easier to follow and share celebrity tweets than it is to memorize the words of Jesus.

I pondered that song for a while. Sometimes, after a church service wraps up and I walk back into my daily life, I feel so disconnected. My mental picture of the God inside the church walls doesn't always seem to fit in the world of terrorist attacks, racism, political upheavals, bullying, and the daily hustle to make a living. It feels like there's an invisible line between the spiritual world and the physical world.

Have you ever felt this way? Have you had a hard time seeing the God of the Bible in the halls of your school, in the place where you work, or in the world around you?

You know what happens when we keep the God part of our life separate from the rest of our life? We limit our experiences of God to the church and we miss out on his work in the world. We become two different people—the Christian for a few hours every week, and the non-Christian for the rest of the time.

This saddens me because I don't think the world can see the light of Christ in us when we live fractured lives like that. As believers, we are called to be disciples of Christ. "Don't you know that friendship with the world means enmity against God?" says James 4:4.

I don't think the world can see the light of Christ in us when we live fractured lives.

"Therefore, anyone who chooses to be a friend of the world becomes an enemy of God." If J. Cole's song is right and we are more friends to the world than we are to Christ, then we make ourselves enemies of God—blocked from seeing his work in us and isolated from his love. It's not enough to try to squeeze God into our spare time. We can't make Jesus fit into our lifestyle. The only way to love God and to know his love for us is to give him total control of our lives.

The world makes us concerned about pleasing others, about things like keeping up with trends and making sure we're in the popular crowd. But God pulls out the best in us, he lifts our focus up to things that matter for the long-term, like getting to know God and helping people. We can't allow ourselves to be so comfortable with our culture that we fit in without thinking, that our lives look just like those who don't know God at all. Instead, God calls us to fix all our attention on him so that rather than being friends of the world, we can show the world who God is.

Where is your attention? Is it focused on fitting in with the world or is it set on following God? If you had to think hard about your answer, you're probably trying to squeeze him into your life rather than giving him your first priority. If you consider yourself a believer and follower of Christ, it's time to give him total control. Matthew 6:33 (NLT) says, "Seek the Kingdom of God above all else, and live righteously, and he will give you everything you need." But remember, this doesn't mean we get to make deals with God. God doesn't work like that—he doesn't trade a little faith and a little time inside a church building for an easy life. He's not a vending machine. God wants all of you, and because he loves you, he will take care of you. We are far more than people of comfort. We are people of the living God.

So don't leave your faith behind when you leave church. Don't lock your heart away from God when you go about your day. The world is full of Christians who look exactly like the rest of the world, who are half in and half out. But we have a higher calling. Instead, surrender your heart to him and invite him into every minute, every second of your day. Be all in. If you do, you will see him work, you'll hear his voice, and you'll know his love.

Life is not perfect, and I never expect it will be. But I can tell you that ever since I gave God total control of my life, things are a lot better. I still encounter the typical everyday challenges we all face, but I know that with God on my side, I can make it through anything life throws at me. If I keep my attention on following God, the difficulties I face are opportunities to show the world who God is.

It's a constant struggle to keep our attention on God, especially because the world shouts at us so loudly and constantly. But we are more than humans living in this world—we are children of God, and the choices we make today ripple into eternity.

CHALLENGE

Spend a few minutes in prayer today. Go somewhere private and quiet where you are able to focus. First, think through every area of your life—family, sports, school, friends, special talents, your finances, thoughts, hopes, dreams and desires, your weaknesses and flaws, the things you struggle with, the things that you're most proud of, and the things you are ashamed of. Tell God that each of these areas are his to use for his glory. Completely surrender. Then ask God to renew your mind and transform your heart to be more like Christ's. Ask him to open your eyes to his presence as you go about your day.

5

Ambassadors for Christ

So we are Christ's ambassadors; God is making his appeal through us. We speak for Christ when we plead, "Come back to God!" For God made Christ, who never sinned, to be the offering for our sin, so that we could be made right with God through Christ.

2 CORINTHIANS 5:20-21 (NLT)

Think for a minute about the clothes you wear, the brands you like, the accessories you buy. Everybody has a style, even those who make a point not to have a style. What kind of lifestyle do you represent?

We all collect brands, slogans, and labels around our personalities like armor. They tell the world what we want others to think about us. When we step out the door, we show the world the side of us we want to be known for. Maybe you are the athlete, the musician, the smart kid, or the artist. Maybe you want to be known for being funny, or caring, or hardworking. We can't help but represent who we are or who we want to be. It's part of being human.

We represent brands and trends so easily when they change from season to season, but so often we don't give much thought to representing what really matters.

The dictionary defines the word *ambassador* as a person who acts as a representative or promoter of a specified activity. Steph Curry, Tim Tebow, Tony Dungy, Manny Pacquiao, Allyson Felix, and many other athletes are not just ambassadors of the professional sports they play. They can often be seen honoring God on and off the field, court, ring, etc. They use their talent, fame, and voice as a platform to be ambassadors for Christ.

It's tempting to think that the role of ambassador is not very important for people who aren't famous or who don't have massive social media followings. You might ask, *what difference does it make to be an ambassador if no one listens or sees?* I tell you this, though—it makes all the difference in the world. See, God didn't say that only the famous should be ambassadors. He called each one of us to represent him right where we are. You have a level of influence that Steph Curry and Tim Tebow don't. You have direct access to your parents, siblings, friends, classmates, and coworkers, and you can challenge, encourage, inspire, love, and converse with them in a way no one else can. As children of God, we are Christ's ambassadors. We must be sure we are representing him well from any platform that he has given us to use—no matter how small it seems.

God didn't say that only the famous should be ambassadors. He called each one of us to represent him right where we are.

Paul says, "For the love of Christ controls us, because we have concluded this: that one has died for all, therefore all have died; and he died for all, that those who live might no longer live for themselves but for him who for their sake died and was raised" (2 Corinthians 5:14–15, ESV). This verse reminds us that our lives are not our own. We have been saved, so we no longer live just for ourselves. We have a mission and a responsibility to represent what Christ did for us.

So now that we are Christians, we cannot go back to our old selves. We cannot keep promoting the wrong team. We have been made new, we have a much more important calling than we realize. Being an ambassador of Christ isn't just about posting a verse every once in a while. It's a full commitment. Think about a professional athlete: they orient their whole life around being the best ambassador they can for their team. This means eating the right foods, sleeping well, training and practicing, listening to their coach, being self-aware, and working to strengthen their weaknesses. In the same way, a true Christ ambassador is a walking picture of what the gospel looks like.

An ambassador is never ashamed of their home team. We need to boldly represent God in the public eye so that others will desire to come to know him. Remember, God doesn't worry about how popular or famous or influential people are. He can use anyone to spread his word. He'll use preachers, teachers, entertainers, and pro athletes to make himself known. But he'll also use you! If you don't think God can use you, then your view of him is too small. So don't be shy or embarrassed. Be bold, because you've been entrusted with the greatest message the world has ever heard.

> If you don't think God can use you, then your view of him is too small.

This is all great, you might be saying, but what does living like an ambassador actually look like day to day? Just like on a sports team, you have to show up for practice and for games. You've got to go to church and spend time with other Christians so that you can learn and be encouraged, and in turn encourage others. You train by praying, reading the Bible, and listening to good teaching.

You can tell you are an ambassador of Christ by the joy and peace you bring to your family. You are an ambassador if you challenge your friends when they participate in a negative activity because of peer pressure. You are an ambassador if your goal is to bring truth, healing, joy, and peace to every interaction. And just like you do when your favorite team wins a big game, you celebrate by spreading the good news.

REFLECT

Think about how you live your life. What kind of impression do you give in the following areas: your interactions with non-believers, your social media and Internet posts, and your attitude at school, work, or among your family and friends? If you were to ask one of your friends what they think you're most passionate about—what you live your life for— what do you think they would say?

Let God use you to represent his kingdom. Spend a few minutes in prayer today, remembering that everything you do, say, and think will either draw people to God or push them away from him. Ask God for the courage to rep him well in every area of your life.

6

A Battle of Choices

The sinful nature wants to do evil, which is just the opposite of what the Spirit wants. And the Spirit gives us desires that are the opposite of what the sinful nature desires. These two forces are constantly fighting each other, so you are not free to carry out your good intentions.

GALATIANS 5:17 (NLT)

How many times have you heard someone say something like, "I'm young and I want to have as much fun as I can before I become an adult. God will forgive me later." How many times have you thought those words yourself?

At this time in your life, you're figuring out the difference between what you *want* to do and what you *should* do. Sometimes, there's a big difference between the two. Doing what we want is always the immediate, easy choice. It's fun, and it satisfies our desires. And doing what we should do can often feel like the opposite. I wish doing what was right all the time wasn't so hard. If doing what was right was easy, there would be a lot more good in the world.

The older you get, the more complicated things become. It's not always easy to tell what is good and what is bad, what is right and what is wrong. And knowing the difference between good and bad doesn't mean you are actually making the right choices. There are times when every choice we make seems to be the wrong one, and we feel guilty no matter what we do.

Way back in the beginning of the world, God told Adam and Eve not to eat of the Tree of the Knowledge of Good and Evil. They did, and that one act brought sin into the world. We feel the pain of that choice today. But it wasn't just the fact Adam and Eve disobeyed God. When Adam and Eve ate the fruit of that tree, they gained knowledge before they were ready. They ruined their innocence with too much information but not enough wisdom to know how to use that knowledge wisely.

Like Adam and Eve, we sometimes have a hard time thinking through all the consequences in order to know which choice is ultimately good and which is ultimately bad. Not every decision will change the course of our lives, but many of them do. And if a choice isn't simple, if the right option isn't immediately obvious, we may feel stuck trying to determine how our futures will be impacted by the decisions we make. Add all the other voices and factors—like cultural traditions, family expectations, and peer pressure—and it's no wonder we have a hard time knowing what is right.

Society often makes fun of people who try to make good choices; we hear this message every day. The world tells us that God's rules don't matter so much and that we should just do what we want. But, as much as this seems like the easiest choice at first, it ends up being the hardest choice to live with. It's tempting to think that only the huge sins harm our relationship with God—like stealing. Little white lies here and there can't be that important, can they? But the truth is that all sin separates us from God. It does not matter how good of a person you think you are or how carefully you try to live your life. We are all still sinners who have fallen short of God's holiness, and only his forgiveness can make us right again.

Like me, you probably try to do the right thing most of the time. But trying to do the right thing can get tricky and confusing really fast. That's because our minds and decisions are strongly influenced by our sinful nature. We have a habit of sinning, even without realizing what we're doing. It's built into our bodies, minds, and hearts.

If you are tempted to think you are the only one that might be struggling to make the right choices, don't be fooled. Look at what Paul says: "I don't really understand myself, for I want to do what is right, but I don't do it. Instead, I do what I hate . . . I want to do what is good, but I don't . . . I have discovered this principle of life—that when I want to do what is right, I inevitably do what is wrong . . . Oh, what a miserable person I am! Who will free me from this life that is dominated by sin and death? Thank God! The answer is in Jesus Christ our Lord" (Romans 7:15–25, NLT). I often find myself rereading these verses as I fight to resist giving in to my sinful nature.

How do we beat this sinful nature and make the right choices? There are three simple steps you can take right now. First: know yourself. If you realize you always make bad decisions at a certain place, with a certain group of people, or during a specific activity, don't put yourself in that position again.

Second: confess. Tell God your sin. Admitting to the wrong, and humbly asking for forgiveness, replaces the effect of sin in your life with the power of God's love and forgiveness.

Third, spend time with God. Keep doing devotions, keep praying, keep hanging out with other Christians. Exposing yourself to God's righteousness strengthens your ability to overcome temptations and choose the right path.

We have to remember that God's Word is truth, and living opposite of the truth is sin and has consequences. God's desire is for each of us to be holy as he is holy, and he doesn't ask us to do anything he hasn't given us the power to accomplish. It's hard. I know it's hard. But remember that you're not alone. 2 Peter 1:3 says that "his divine power has given us everything we need for a godly life." God is with you, helping and guiding you in every choice.

WRITE

As you journal today, reflect on the areas in your life where you struggle the most to do the right thing. Why do you think it's so hard? Consider how using the three steps we talked about earlier can help you avoid sin in the future. Pray and ask God to give you wisdom to make the right choices— even if they're hard. Remember, it is never too late to start making good decisions.

7

God-Given Calling

He called you to this through our gospel, that you might share in the glory of our Lord Jesus Christ.

2 THESSALONIANS 2:14

I remember the day I realized I needed to change. I had experienced a lot of hard things—I watched my dad fight cancer, I'd gotten injured and had to give up the sport I had focused my whole future on, I'd fallen in love and broken up, and I'd gone through some really dark months when I struggled with depression.

By the time I came to this particular day, I was just coasting, just surviving. I didn't expect much from life anymore and I didn't expect much from myself because, time and time again, I'd seen all my efforts disintegrated by fluke incidents. I thought it didn't matter what I did, how hard I worked, or even if I had a calling to live for. Because life could simply throw a crazy curveball at me—like my dad's cancer or my basketball injury—and everything would fall apart.

I remember walking across campus, talking on the phone with a friend from home. I was bragging about something I had done that I had no business doing, let alone bragging about. And then, mid-sentence, I heard God speak to me as clear as a bell. In my mind, I heard him say, "Dana, that's not who I made you to be. I have given you a higher calling."

I hung up the phone right away. I went straight to my dorm, dropped to my knees, and asked God for his forgiveness. I told God and myself that I was going to be a better man.

Ever since I made that choice, I've done my best to live up to it. Oh, for sure, I still mess up. I still go through ups and downs, but I am slowly learning that it really does matter what we do and how we act.

Paul is one of my favorite people in the Bible. I love that God took a murderer and used him to lead so many people to Christ. When I read about Paul's life in the book of Acts, I'm reminded that God was fully aware of Paul's rough past. God knows everything. He's never surprised by our failings or our mess. God had a plan to use Paul's life for good, just like he has a plan to use mine and yours for good too. He gave Paul a special calling. Once Paul realized he wasn't meant to be a persecutor of the church but a defender of Christ, his whole life changed.

God knows everything. He's never surprised by our failings or our mess.

It's hard to believe that God chose us even before he formed the earth. He knew Paul, me, and you before we were even a thought in our parents' minds. Psalm 139:15–16 says, "My frame was not hidden from you when I was made in the secret place, when I was woven together in the depths of the earth. Your eyes saw my unformed body; all the days ordained for me were written in your book before one of them came to be." Before the stars existed, before the oceans and mountains came to be, God had a plan and a calling for each of us.

Paul understood that we're not just called to be good people. Following God is so much more than that. Ephesians 1:4–5 says, "For he chose us in him before the creation of the world to be holy and blameless in his sight. In love he predestined us for adoption to sonship through Jesus Christ." God created us to be his sons and daughters. When we realize that we're children of God, we can't coast through our days as if it doesn't matter. If you met the son or daughter of the president of the United States, you would expect them to be gracious, polite, and to treat others well, right? Because they're not just a kid; they represent their father. As sons and daughters of God, it really does matter what we do, what we think, and how we act because we represent our Father. God didn't just give us a job to do—he gave us a completely different way to live.

I know I'll mess up again. It's an unfortunate part of being human. But I'm more than just a human. I'm a child of God, and I know that God is working in me, making me a better man and a better follower of Christ. And one day, when I die, I'll see my Father face to face, and all my mistakes will be forgotten, and I'll feel his big, strong arms around me. But for now, my goal on earth is to live every day in a way that makes him proud.

REFLECT

Take some time today to reflect on your thoughts, the words you speak, and the things you do. Do you think your life looks like the life of a son or daughter of a powerful king? Why or why not? Journal about what being a child of God means to you. How does it change you as a person? Does it change how you treat others around you? How does it affect the way you think about God?

8

Are You Willing?

For from him and through him and
for him and for him are all things. To him be the
glory forever! Amen.

ROMANS 11:36

Do you know how the disciples came to follow
Jesus in the first place? Matthew 4:18–22 tells
how Jesus walked on the shore of the Sea of Galilee one
day. Fishermen worked on the beach or fished in their
boats out on the water. Jesus saw two brothers, Peter
and Andrew, casting their nets in the water and he said,
"Come, follow me and I will send you out to fish for
people." And immediately, Peter and Andrew left their
nets and followed him.

Can you imagine making this kind of major life
change so quickly? I have a feeling that if Jesus came up
to me and said, "Hey, stop what you're doing and follow
me," I would have about a thousand questions. But that's
not all. A little way down the beach, Jesus found two

other brothers, James and John. They sat in a boat with their dad, mending their nets. And Jesus called out to them, and just like the first two, James and John stopped what they were doing, and left the boat and even their father to follow Jesus.

The culture was different back then for James, John, Peter, and Andrew. We don't have the same kind of teacher/student relationship that they knew. For the Israelites, if a student wanted to become a disciple, they went to the teacher and asked permission to learn from him. But instead, Jesus chose his own disciples and asked them to follow him. And what's more, these guys weren't scholars or students of Judaism; they were just regular people going about their day like usual. To these ordinary fishermen, being called by a teacher of God was an astounding thing. At that time, Jesus was only starting to be recognized as a teacher. He hadn't done many miracles; he wasn't famous yet. And these four guys probably weren't much older than you or me. And yet they wanted to know God so much that when a teacher offered to show them who God was, they dropped everything, left everyone, and followed him with no hesitation. When I think about these men, I can't help but ask myself, what am I willing to do? How far am I willing to go? Am I willing to surrender everything for his glory?

Not too long after Jesus called the four brothers to follow him, Jesus talked with another young man. This guy had memorized Scripture and was trying to live a good life the best he knew how. But the young man wanted eternal life in heaven and knew that doing a few good things wasn't enough to achieve that. So he asked Jesus what else he needed to do. Jesus told him, "One thing you lack. Go, sell everything you have and give to the poor, and you will have treasure in heaven. Then come, and follow me" (Mark 10:21). But the young man became sad because he was really wealthy, and giving it all away meant a drastic change in his lifestyle. Would you be willing to let go of your comfort, your money, your way of living, and risk it all for the amazing gift of knowing God? It's not an easy thing to imagine, right? Our culture teaches us to value our possessions and our wealth, but Jesus teaches us to value the people around us and the things we believe in.

We've talked about Paul's story and how God called him to teach people all around the world about Jesus. Paul did so, but it wasn't easy. He gave up his life of luxury and his status of being one of the most respected religious leaders of his day to become a radical follower of Jesus, often without a place to stay the night. Five times, he was arrested and whipped with thirty-nine lashes. He was stoned once and beaten with rods three times. He was even shipwrecked. Not to mention all the nights he spent cold, braving severe weather on his frequent travels, or times when he went hungry or thirsty. Everything Paul had, he gave up to God. He willingly suffered for God's glory because Jesus first suffered for him. He knew it was worth it.

Paul knew his mission would never be easy, yet he willingly endured great trials to know God. You may not be facing the same things Paul faced. You may not be beaten or lashed with a whip for talking about Christ.

But like Paul, the disciples, and every other follower of Christ, Jesus has chosen you, and there may come a day when you need to let go of your life as you know it. Maybe your health will be threatened. Maybe, like me, you will need to let go of your plans for your future.

Jesus has chosen you, and there may come a day when you need to let go of your life as you know it.

Maybe God is asking you to give something up right now. Are you willing to break off that unhealthy relationship? Would you stop that bad habit? Can you put someone else first before you get what you want? How far are you willing to go?

I don't know what God is calling you to do, but I do know that he asks all

We need to be willing to risk it all for the surpassing worth of knowing Christ Jesus.

of us to be ready to give up our lives for him so that we may experience his love. We need to hold our lives—all our dreams, hopes, words, thoughts, deeds, family members, friends, talents, health—in an open hand. We can't be like the young rich man who was too comfortable to take the next step in following Jesus. Instead, like Paul, we need to be willing to risk it all for the surpassing worth of knowing Christ Jesus.

WRITE

Journal about what it means to you to hold everything in your life in an open hand. What is the hardest thing to let go of? Why do you think it is so hard? Is God asking you to give anything up today? How much are you willing to let go of for Christ? After you think and write about these questions, pray and ask God to help you to be willing to risk it all for the one who risked it all for you.

9

Finding Time

How can a young person stay on the path of purity? By living according to your word.

PSALM 119:9

When I was a student, I felt like I was always running late and forgetting important assignments. It was hard to keep track of my homework deadlines. I would wake up late for practice or class, and that would set me back for the rest of the day. Then I'd stay up late hoping to squeeze in everything I needed to do. And of course, because of the late night, I would sleep past my alarm, and around and around I'd go. It was an exhausting cycle.

In our culture, everyone is always rushing around. We are all so busy. We are even proud of how busy we are. We brag about it to our friends because it makes us feel important and needed. And despite all the devices we have to track time, we are still not able to manage it as well as we'd like. But it only gets worse from here. The older you get, the less and less time you have and the more and more things you will have to do.

And somehow, in between all this rushing around, we need to build in time with God. But I'll be honest with you, when I'm late for something or super busy, the first thing I skip is my time with God. I opt to catch up on something else that day. I bet you've done the same thing a time or two. Maybe we skip it because it's hard to sit still and practice listening to God when we have a hundred tasks and worries running through our mind. It can be hard to focus on learning something new when you feel pressed for time.

But what happens when we do miss this time with God each day? We may not notice anything different the first time we skip, or even the sixth time. But a week without time with God? A month? Our minds lose the balance and perspective that comes with praying and reading Scripture. When we deprive ourselves of this time, our souls become distraught and stressed, and we aren't able to be close to God in the way we want to be, the way we *need* to be.

Think about one of your close friends. How long could you go without hanging out or talking to them before you're no longer friends? If you never asked them how they were doing or listened to what they were thinking about, would they know that you cared about them? We all have a friendship that just faded away because we lost touch with each other. That's what happens when a relationship isn't given the time it needs. It's important to make time for friends, to hang out with each other.

> Satan specializes in keeping us busy so that we won't have time to be with the one who made our souls.

And it's even more important to carve out time in your schedule to hang out with the most important person in all your life—the one who protects you and loves you no matter what.

So why is it so hard to find the time? The Bible says that we have a real enemy, Satan, and he doesn't want you to spend time with God. He specializes in keeping us busy so that we won't have time to be with the one who made our souls. The sad thing is that he doesn't have to work very hard at it, because we humans are easily distracted. It's hard for us to manage our time well, to prioritize our relationship with God, and to stay focused on what's important. As long as we're distracted by things that *seem* important in the moment but actually aren't important in the long run, then our enemy is winning and we are lost. As Psalm 39:4–5 says, life is fleeting. We don't have all the time in the world, so we need to learn to be careful and intentional with the time that we do have.

> Jesus not only deserves our time and attention, but he longs to spend time with us, his friends.

Busyness can never be an excuse for not making time to be with God. Jesus not only deserves our time and attention, but he longs to spend time with us, his friends. He has things to teach you and show you and say to you. He can't wait to be with you.

PRACTICE

We can't just hope to get better at managing our time. Wishing to get better won't get us very far. We have to build time with God into our schedule and make it a habit. So how do you do that?

- **Prioritize**: This time is just as important as it is for you to eat. Without food, your body dies. Without time with God, your soul dies.

- **Plan**: Think about your schedule and all the things you need to do in the day. What period makes the most sense to set aside for God? Look for a twenty-minute window at the same time every day. Maybe it's first thing in the morning right as you roll out of bed. Or maybe it's at night before your head hits the pillow. For me, personally, I'm usually so tired at night that I forget. So I make sure I spend a few minutes reading and praying first thing in the morning. This also helps me get my mind around what's really important before I start my day.

- **Stay focused**: It takes about two months of daily practice to make a habit. Make sure you stay strong for the first few weeks. Don't let anything hinder you from getting with Jesus every day. If you need a reminder, set one in your cell phone or write a note and place it somewhere you'll be sure to see it. If noise distracts you, close the door and put your cell phone on silent. If someone asks you to do something while you're in the middle of reading your Bible, tell them you will help them out as soon as you're finished.

- **Make it fun**: We dread things that seem boring. But trust me, Jesus isn't boring. So if we're bored with him, we're missing something. Read a chapter of the Bible, but read a book that you haven't read before. Then spend a few minutes praying and listening to Jesus. I know some people who read a passage and then draw it as a way to think about it in more detail. Others memorize verses. Some walk in the mornings and pray as they go. You can always use a devotional, like the one you're reading, to help guide your time with God. I tend to read a chapter or a devotional and then journal my thoughts, observations, and prayers. I like to be able to look back and see the journey I've gone through. Be creative, change it up. But make sure to spend time with Jesus.

10

Choose with Caution

Walk with the wise and become
wise, for a companion of fools suffers
harm.
PROVERBS 13:20

I'm sure you've heard the saying, "You become who you hang out with." My parents said it often when I was a kid, but it never meant much to me. My mom and dad were very specific about who my siblings and I spent time with. Some people we knew considered them strict and others just considered it good parenting because my parents were intentional and cared about our friendships. My mom and dad understood the power that friends have on a person and wanted to teach us to be careful of the company we kept. They specifically emphasized one verse when we were going into high school and again when we headed off to college: 1 Corinthians 15:33, which says, "Do not be misled: 'Bad company corrupts good character.'"

Bad company corrupts good character.

At the time, though, I didn't really get this verse. I figured that my friends would do what they wanted and I would do what I wanted. And I wanted to be liked, I wanted to be popular. Who doesn't? All of our lives, we feel the pressure to fit in, to be liked. I felt that pressure especially hard in school.

Then, during my first few years of college, I found myself hanging with a crowd who had different values than I did. I didn't think that friends really influenced me so much, and believed I could fit in without having to compromise myself. I thought I was strong enough to keep my values intact, but it wasn't long before I found myself slipping, doing the same things my friends were doing. I started partying more and going to church less. I followed my friends into everything I was raised to stay away from. I went along for two years like I didn't know any better. Then God woke me up. In an earlier chapter, I told the story about the phone call, where I was bragging about something I shouldn't have, and God convicted me about it. He reminded me that he had given me a calling—not to worry about being liked or popular, but to follow Jesus.

I realized I was only fooling myself by thinking that the people I spent the most time with weren't influencing my life. I knew I needed to make some deliberate choices about my friendships. Like Proverbs 12:26 says, "The righteous choose their friends carefully, but the way of the wicked leads them astray."

I needed to make a change, so I transferred to a Christian college. I settled in quickly and became captain of the basketball team. I noticed some students looked up to me and I suddenly realized I needed a good group of friends who would push me to be a better person, someone worth looking up to. I started hanging with people who challenged and helped each other. It was such a better group to be with. Unlike my old friends, I felt I could really trust these people. Seeing how these new friends had each other's backs caused me to start being more intentional about who I shared my time with.

I learned a lot from those friends—what to look for in a friend and how to be a good friend. I learned that a good friend doesn't lie, spread rumors, gossip, or bully. Good friends don't push you into doing something wrong or below your values. Instead, they help you when you are struggling, give wise advice, cover your back, tell you the truth instead of flattering you, and challenge you to get closer to Christ.

When you consider the friends you hang out with the most, do they match the description of a good friend? If they don't, then you will need to reevaluate who you are giving your time and attention to. Perhaps it's time to back off on some relationships because they are doing more harm than good in your life. Now this doesn't mean to be hateful or rude to them. You should still be friendly and caring, because that is the kind of unconditional friend Jesus is to us. In fact, you may be able to help and encourage them. Backing up a little simply means that those are people you don't spend a ton of time with. Invite them to hang out with a group of your good friends so that you both have the support of healthy friendships. Or meet them for lunch or coffee, giving them intentional time for an hour or two and then giving the rest of your time to other things.

Here's the real challenge: think about what kind of friend you are. Do you match the description of a good friend? If not, what do you think you need to change to get back on track? Proverbs 27:17 says, "As iron sharpens iron, so one person sharpens another." Make sure you are being the type of friend that you would want—someone who can be trusted, who respects others, who sharpens your friends with gentle challenges and encouragements.

Know that if you ever feel lonely or like you don't have any good friends, you can trust that Jesus will always have your back. He is always with you. He gives you that uncomfortable feeling if you're about to do something wrong, he reminds you of good advice to share with others, and he helps you love others well. Most importantly, he loves you unconditionally. None of us will ever find a better friend than Jesus.

REFLECT

Like we talked about above, think about your friend crew right now. Ask yourself if you have a good, healthy friend group that you are proud of. Consider how you can be a better friend. Is there something you need to say or do for someone else today?

Memorize or write this verse down to commit it to memory: "Do not be misled: 'Bad company corrupts good character'" (1 Corinthians 15:33).

11

Imitation

And you should imitate me, just as I
imitate Christ.
1 CORINTHIANS 11:1 (NLT)

From movie stars to athletes, people spend their life-
times imitating and following other people. Imitation
is built into our nature as a survival instinct and a learning
strategy. We even do it without noticing. You can see this
in our culture—from fashion trends to political debates.
Patterning your life after someone else isn't a bad thing
in itself; however, there is a great danger in following the
wrong person. Because if we're not careful, we will end up
dangerously far away from where, and who, we want to be.

As a college athlete, I spent a lot of time studying
players that I wanted to base my game after. I wanted to
grow my potential, so I looked to professional players to
show me what was possible. But it was important to me
to follow players who were not only good at the game of
basketball, they also lived their lives well off the court.

There are a ton of players who are known for their amazing skills but who, unfortunately, lack character. They might be able to do some remarkable tricks, but they let anger get the best of them, or they're unable to handle losses, or they let addictions rule their lives. Those were not the players I wanted to follow. Paul told the Corinthian Christians to imitate him as he imitated Christ, and I took his instructions seriously. So I found myself following and learning from players like Steph Curry, LeBron James, and Tim Tebow. Each of these players have been good role models in sports and in life.

Most importantly, I try to pattern my life after Jesus, which is much easier said than done. Jesus said, "I have set you an example that you should do as I have done for you" (John 13:15). This is our main purpose in life, but it's a hard thing to accomplish. One of the reasons why it is so difficult is because it takes wisdom and practice to know how to follow the example of Jesus in our world today. I'm sure you've noticed that our world is much different than the world Jesus grew up in. So it helps to have human role models who show us how to live like Jesus day to day. Hebrews 13:7 says, "Remember your leaders, who spoke the word of God to you. Consider the outcome of their way of life and imitate their faith." God knows we need extra help and encouragement, so he places people in our lives, faith leaders, who set an example of what it looks like to follow God in real life. One of Steph Curry's role models is his dad, and LeBron James listens carefully to his mom's advice. They've come to trust in their parents' wisdom and support.

I am lucky enough to have my own dad as a mentor.

It takes wisdom and practice to know how to follow the example of Jesus in our world today.

I know so many people don't have a dad to teach them about life, but I hope you have someone who can fill this role for you. And keep in mind, I don't *always* agree with my dad. Sometimes we have different ideas about the right thing to do or how to do it. But my dad always has my back. I trust him to help me see what's most important, what's at risk, and to point out any dangers I haven't noticed yet. He always has wise advice, encouragement, or a good question for me to think about.

Role models don't have to be parents, though. Tim Tebow looks to his parents, but also a handful of other professional athletes. A role model can be a coach, a youth pastor, a college professor, an aunt, uncle, cousin, a teacher, an older sibling, or the parent of one of your friends. Like my sports role models, a good role model needs to do life well on and off the court, in and out of church, at work and at home. A good role model will be trying to live their life after Christ. No one is perfect, but you want to mirror your life after people who are living in a way that honors God.

As much as I look up to Steph Curry and LeBron James, I've found the best role models are people who you can meet with and talk with on a regular basis. A celebrity can give you an idea of what is possible and they can inspire you, but what is more helpful is a mentor who understands your story, who understands you and where you're trying to go, and who can be there for you any day.

Find a role model you can meet with regularly. You might already have someone in your life who inspires you. Ask them questions about life, relationships, religion, school, and the future. Learn everything you can from them so that their knowledge and experience can help you as you grow. A good role model helps you imitate Christ because they break down spiritual principles into real-life scenarios for you. For example, you can read about loving your neighbor as yourself, but it is more powerful if you watch someone go out of their way to care for their friends and family.

Recognize who that role model is in your life and listen carefully to what they say. Actually follow their advice. You'll learn a lot just by watching what they do, listening to what they say, and asking them questions about why they do what they do. Especially watch them when they're

The more you learn how to imitate a role model, the more you'll know how to follow Jesus.

going through tough times. I've learned so much from watching my dad in his fight against cancer. Even on his worst days, he taught me how to be gracious and to trust God when you don't know what the future holds.

And here's the secret: The more you learn how to imitate a role model, the more you'll know how to follow Jesus. Because Jesus is our true model and our goal for a life of joy and abundance.

REFLECT

Whether we realize it or not, we naturally try to imitate other people. Who have you been following? Are you imitating someone who sets a good example? Think about the person God has placed in your life to help you grow. Try to be more intentional about watching that person and asking them good questions. Ask God to help you learn how to follow Christ and the role models he's placed in your life.

12

Confidence in Christ

So God has given both his promise and his oath. These two things are unchangeable because it is impossible for God to lie. Therefore, we who have fled to him for refuge can have great confidence as we hold to the hope that lies before us.

HEBREWS 6:18 (NLT)

Many of us have a hard time trusting other people, and for good reason. Whether it's a friend who let us down one too many times, a parent who's no longer there for us, or a coach or teacher who ended up doing more harm for us than help, other people have hurt us. To protect ourselves from more pain, we learn quickly to be wary and skeptical of people.

I felt this struggle even when I was very young. I had a hard time trusting others and letting them in, so I spent a lot of time alone. That instinct follows me even to this day. Often, I end up translating this same kind of human distrust to my relationship with God as well. I fear that God will somehow leave or forget about me or let me down, just like other people in my life. We all struggle to trust that we are actually liked and loved by God.

I am reminded of the promise God gave in Deuteronomy 31:6, where he says he will never leave us nor forsake us. But the truth is, sometimes it seems like God doesn't show up, like he has left us. Have you ever felt this way? Sometimes God is quiet, or our emotions tell us that he's far away. We all have this deep, primal fear that God doesn't truly want to be with us.

But here's what I'm learning: We cannot let our human fears define our understanding of God.

> We cannot let our human fears define our understanding of God.

Though God made us, he is not human. So we cannot expect him to act the same way we do. Humans are inconsistent, but God is not. This is a hard concept for us because, as humans, you and I are used to change. Our bodies change as we grow older, the weather changes, we change grades then schools and then jobs. But God doesn't change. He is the same today as he was a thousand years ago, and the same as a million years ago. In James 1:17, God says that he is the father of lights and there is no shifting shadow in him. No shifting shadow, no darkness, no falsehood, no wrongness. God is all good. And Numbers 23:19 says, "God is not human, that he should lie, not a human being, that he should change his mind. Does he speak and then not act? Does he promise and not fulfill?" God is all good; he never lies. So when he makes a promise, you can trust that he will keep it.

If one of my friends lets me down, it wouldn't be fair for me to distrust my other friend or treat them as if they've hurt me too. It's the same with God. It's not fair for us to treat God as if he has left us or abandoned us, because he hasn't. Of course, we'll never understand him perfectly—God is mysterious sometimes. But we know this for sure: God is good and his love never fails. Friends come and go and families change, but God is steadfast. God is the only consistency in our lives—people will fail you whether they mean to or not. However, we can always rely on Christ.

Friends come and go and families change, but God is steadfast.

None of us are perfect, and sometimes our fear and distrust of others get the best of us. But when we fully realize just how faithful and trustworthy God is, that truth frees us from our fear. We can face all sorts of terrible things when we believe that the powerful God of the universe has our back.

The more I learn about God, the more I realize that God is trustworthy. That doesn't mean it's always easy to trust him, but I've seen God be faithful over and over again. I know that everything he does is good and for our good.

In these chaotic times, there is very little we can trust in. People will disappoint or hurt us, even if it wasn't their intention. Friends, siblings, parents, coworkers, and employers will make promises and not be able to keep them. How powerful and comforting it is to know that we are secure in Christ who never fails or wavers. For just as 2 Thessalonians 3:3 says, the Lord is faithful, and he will love and protect you.

WRITE

It's an easy thing to forget how much we can trust God. Life comes at us hard sometimes, and we lose our confidence in our Father. So to help remind yourself of who you can trust, write down these verses from Psalm 91. In your Bible, put a bookmark on the chapter so that you can reference it easily in the future.

"Whoever dwells in the shelter of the Most High will rest in the shadow of the Almighty. I will say of the LORD, 'He is my refuge and my fortress, my God, in whom I trust.'"

PSALM 91:1-2

"'Because he loves me,' says the LORD, 'I will rescue him; I will protect him, for he acknowledges my name. He will call on me, and I will answer him; I will be with him in trouble, I will deliver him and honor him. With long life I will satisfy him and show him my salvation.'"

PSALM 91:14-16

13

Make Your Request Known

And I will do whatever you ask in my name, so that the Father may be glorified in the Son. You may ask me for anything in my name, and I will do it.

JOHN 14:13-14

Do you ever dread praying? If I'm in a group of people, say at a youth group or with some friends, I get nervous about praying because I'm worried I'll say something stupid. (Public praying requires some serious courage!) Other times, I dread praying because I'm afraid that my prayers are useless, that God doesn't hear them.

Being nervous about speaking in public can be easily fixed. A little practice is all it takes. But being afraid that our prayers aren't effective or that God doesn't hear them . . . that's a deeper issue.

As I get older and grow in my faith, I have come to learn that we dread prayer for two reasons.

The first reason is that it's tough to have a dialogue when you feel like you're the only one talking. When we chat with our friends and family, we nod at each other, meet each other's eyes, and ask follow-up questions. We are so used to those social cues that when we don't receive them, we wonder if God is even there at all. But remember, we cannot let our human thinking define our understanding of God. Just because God doesn't respond according to our culture or our traditions, it doesn't mean he isn't there or that he's not listening. The Bible tells us again and again that God does hear the prayers of those who follow him, like 1 Peter 3:12, which says, "For the eyes of the Lord are on the righteous and his ears are attentive to their prayer."

Just think about what prayer really is. Prayer is when we commune and talk with the Holy God and Creator of everything. Much like learning a new language, we need to learn how to talk and listen to God so that we hear and

Prayer is when we commune and talk with the Holy God and Creator of everything.

understand what he is saying. Though it is different than talking with other humans, prayer is not complicated. Simply address your thoughts to God. In fact, not that many words are necessary. Matthew 6 states that we don't need to babble on to God with long sentences, because God knows our needs and our requests even before we ask them. We need to only tell him our request and he hears us.

You can speak to Jesus in your mind or out loud. Or you can journal, describing your thoughts, requests, and experiences to God, and that is prayer. You can sit in silence, your mind focused on being *with* God, and that too is prayer.

Mother Teresa said that prayer is faith. And I find this to be very true. It takes faith to trust that God is listening. But as 1 John 5:14 says, "This is the confidence we have in approaching God: that if we ask anything according to his will, he hears us." Prayer is intimate and it is beautiful. It is you and God coming face to face. You can rest in the fact that God is indeed listening more closely than you can imagine.

The second reason I think we struggle with prayer is that we worry we're wasting our time. Have you ever prayed for something and that something never happened? I have. At those times when I think prayer has let me down, or that it didn't work, I worry that I didn't pray hard enough or that I didn't say the right words. But prayer is not a formula. It's a relationship. And sometimes God says no, or not yet. We may never know why God answers the way he does. But I can look back now, and I am grateful for some of the prayers that weren't answered the way I had wanted. God doesn't just want us to be happy in the moment but to grow to our fullest potential. He sees all things, he knows what's good for us, and sometimes the requests we ask seem right in the moment but aren't the best thing for us in the long run. So sometimes his answer is different than what we hope for. We have to trust that when God says no, it's not because he is cruel, but rather because he is looking out for us. But that doesn't mean you shouldn't pray and ask for something. In fact, the Bible says that if you really want it, ask for it persistently. And God says yes more than we realize.

Even if we receive a no from God, our prayers are never wasted. We may not know what full effect our prayers have, but God uses all things for our good and for his glory.

> Even if we receive a no from God, our prayers are never wasted.

God loves to work with us. It is part of our calling as children of God to partner with him as he loves and heals humanity. And one of the most powerful ways we work with him is through prayer—praying for ourselves and for those around us.

Trust that God does in fact hear you whether you feel his response or not. Have confidence to keep on praying. Philippians 4:5–7 reads, "The Lord is near. Do not be anxious about anything, but in every situation, by prayer and petition, with thanksgiving, present your requests to God. And the peace of God, which transcends all understanding, will guard your hearts and your minds in Christ Jesus."

Make it a practice to pray every day, drawing closer to the God who loves you and wants to work with you.

PRACTICE

The disciples had questions about prayer, and they asked Jesus to teach them how to pray well. Jesus taught them the words below. Say this prayer today in your heart, or write it in your journal. After you finish the praying, sit in silence for a minute or two and try to listen for God's voice. Maybe God will give you a thought, or a verse will come to mind. Maybe you won't hear anything except the peaceful silence of God's presence. Either way, practice listening to the one who loves you.

Our Father in heaven,
hallowed be your name,
your kingdom come,
your will be done,
 on earth as it is in heaven.
Give us today our daily bread.
And forgive us our debts,
 as we also have forgiven our debtors.
And lead us not into temptation,
 but deliver us from the evil one.

MATTHEW 6:9–13

14

Every Thought

Finally, brothers and sisters, whatever
is true, whatever is noble, whatever is
right, whatever is pure, whatever
is lovely, whatever is admirable—if
anything is excellent or praiseworthy—
think about such things.

PHILIPPIANS 4:8

Our minds are not always very reliable. One day,
I'm able to think clearly and remember how much
God has done for me and that I'm loved as his son. And
the next day, I can't stop thinking about how I'm messing everything up, or wondering if God really does love
me at all, or worrying if the future will be okay. Often,
doubts or anxieties about certain situations get the best
of me, and I forget that God has my back. I know it's an
everyday struggle for us all to keep our thoughts on a
healthy track. They so easily spin out of our control.

Peter was a pretty bold follower of Jesus, very

passionate and a bit of a daredevil. But even Peter, as bold as he was, struggled with his thoughts sometimes. In Matthew 14, Jesus sends Peter and the other disciples in a boat to cross the Sea of Galilee. Jesus stayed back to pray through the night until just before dawn. Peter and the disciples were probably exhausted, rowing for hours. Suddenly, Peter saw something on the water coming toward their boat. At first, the disciples freaked out because it looked like a ghost. But Jesus called out and let them know it was him.

Peter, in his typical bold form, said, "Lord, if it's you, tell me to come to you on the water." And Jesus said, "Come." Peter scrambled out of the boat and took one step, then two. He walked on the water like Jesus. But then, Peter noticed the wind blowing and the waves rising and falling, and his thoughts spun out of control. He became afraid and started to sink. Jesus grabbed Peter's hand and pulled him back to safety. Peter was looking right at Jesus, seeing with his own eyes the evidence of the miracle. But even still, his fear and anxiety of drowning got the better of him.

One of the greatest faith leaders in the Bible is Moses. When we think of him, most of us have this mental picture of Moses as a strong old man with a white beard, someone imposing and full of confidence. But that's not who he was when God called him. When God first appeared to Moses and told him that he was sending him to Egypt to lead the Israelites out of slavery, Moses told God that he had the wrong man. Moses worried that no one would listen to him, or that he wouldn't be able to speak well enough. He was afraid that if he did what

God told him to do, people would think he was crazy. God answered each one of Moses's worries and even performed two miracles to remind Moses that he was indeed God. God turned Moses's staff into a snake and then back into a staff again, and then he struck Moses's hand with a disease and then healed it right in front of him. Still, Moses struggled with self-doubt. Eventually, Moses did go to Egypt and he did lead the Israelites out of slavery, but he struggled hard along the way to trust God more than his fears.

Doubts, fears, worries, and anxieties are a normal part of being human. They can even be good because they help us think through all the different scenarios we're facing and they alert us to danger. However, when we give more attention to our fears than to God, we become trapped by our own thoughts. If we give all the power to our own mind, then we are unable to see God's truth and move forward in his light. But when we trust that God is more powerful than our situations and his words are more true than our own thoughts, we are then free to do even the hardest and most courageous of things, knowing God has our back.

God is more powerful than our situations, and his words are more true than our own thoughts.

Notice that in the cases of both Peter and Moses, God wasn't shocked by their mental struggle against fear and doubt. He was patient and reassured them of who he is and of his powerful love for his children. God does the same for us if we bring our thoughts to him. He teaches us to "take captive every thought to make it obedient to Christ" (2 Corinthians 10:5). And we do this by praying about our thoughts.

If your mind is spinning out of control, know that you can always take your thoughts to God. Like Peter, if you're fighting against fear and anxiety, ask God to remind you how powerful he is, and that he's got your back.

If your mind is spinning out of control, know that you can always take your thoughts to God.

Fighting thoughts of doubt and fear is something I deal with on a regular basis. But just like anything else, with practice, it gets easier. The more you include God in your thoughts, praying and asking for his truth to overcome your fear, the more you'll be able to trust in him. So even when you're faced with terrifying storms, you'll be able to confidently stand beside Jesus.

WRITE

Today, journal and write down the fears you struggle against. Put them down on paper— the big fears and the little worries, the terrifying thoughts and your crippling anxieties. You can trust that God understands each and every one of your doubts. Then write this verse at the end of your list: "My sheep listen to my voice; I know them, and they follow me. I give them eternal life, and they shall never perish; no one will snatch them out of my hand" (John 10:27–28).

Then, when you're done, pray and ask God to help you recognize the difference between your thoughts and his voice. And ask him to remind you that he is greater than all things.

15

Don't Look at Me

Let someone else praise you, not
your own mouth—a stranger, not
your own lips.,
PROVERBS 27:2 (NLT)

Social media is amazing. The level of connectivity
we have through social media is unprecedented. We
can constantly keep up with our friends, favorite teams,
celebrities, brands, and stay in the know on what's trend-
ing. But let's be real: we are addicted to the attention
when it comes to our profiles.

Many of us get sucked into mentally cataloging every
like, comment, and follower. We can't go anywhere,
do anything, without at least thinking about snapping
a photo. And when we're not thinking about our own
online presence, we're carefully watching others and
comparing their popularity to our own.

We all feel the pressure to post, to put ourselves out
there and see how many likes we can get, because that is

how we are seen, heard, validated. We're like little kids yelling, "Look at me!" to anyone who will listen. This puts us in a tough situation when we read verses like John 5:44, where Jesus asks his followers, "How can you believe since you accept glory from one another but do not seek the glory that comes from the only God?" If we solely look to other people for glory and validation, then by definition we are not looking to God for those things. But God is the only one who can speak accurately about our identity and self-worth. Though people can say encouraging things, the glory they give is fickle and only lasts a short time. God, though, is not fickle. What he says is absolutely true and trustworthy. We can stake our faith on what he says, we can build our lives on it.

We need to keep that truth in mind when we think about how we use social media. The technology that allows us to be so interconnected with each other is a valuable gift. But it becomes a trap if underneath it all, fueling our addiction, is a craving for personal recognition. In a word, social media is selfish. When we publish a post, I bet very few of us are thinking of how our posts can help someone else. We use social media to make ourselves feel good, we use it to increase our social status. But the Bible teaches us to "do nothing out of selfish ambition or vain conceit. Rather, in humility value others above yourselves" (Philippians 2:3). So, what if we sought to help and encourage others through our social platforms? Some of my friends who are closely connected with ministries use their posts to celebrate when a child is adopted or a human trafficking victim is rescued. I love it when individuals post about friends or family members, publicly honoring someone who's important to them. And I'm personally encouraged when people honestly share their struggles and the lessons they're learning about following God. Authenticity is hard to come by online, and it carries a powerful effect.

If our motive behind every post is to get attention and recognition from other people, then we lose recognition from God. But if you are humble and keep your focus on following God, then the one who sees all hidden things will reward you.

What if we sought to help and encourage others through our social platforms?

One major gift that our media-driven culture misses out on is the sacredness of the hidden moment. By that I mean the little bits of time you spend here and there doing ordinary things—chores, homework, getting ready for the day. These quiet moments are ignored because social media only values the extraordinary, the glamorous, the applause-worthy events. But God has a special place in his heart for the moments in our lives when no one else sees us, when no one else is applauding. It's in these moments we are our true selves—no likes, no filters. He uses these times when we are undistracted to connect and be with us.

Our integrity is also developed in these hidden moments. Taking out the trash or loading the dishwasher

But God has a special place in his heart for the unseen moments in our lives when no one else sees us, when no one else is applauding.

isn't post-worthy, but it's through times like these that we love those we're closest to. Deciding not to lash out at a sibling or holding back road rage isn't something you can take a selfie of, but God sees you trying to be a better person. A serious conversation about your friend's struggle with depression or how they're handling their parents' divorce isn't something you make public. But being there with them during that time is exactly how you can share God's comfort. How sad would it be if you missed that opportunity because you were on your phone? It's in these hidden moments that God is working in you to help you grow.

Social media is imbedded in our culture; whole industries exist now because of it. And please, don't hear me say that social technology is bad through and through. It's not. But just like in everything we do, we need to be aware of our motives. Do you use social media to chase after the recognition and fame, or will you use it in a way that glorifies God?

REFLECT

Pull up your social media history and look at the kind of posts you publish. What do people see? Can people see love in your posts, or do they see pride? Consider ways you can use your social media platform to encourage, challenge, and share God's truth and love with others. Maybe that means being more honest, posting your real thoughts and feelings so that others going through the same things don't feel alone. Or maybe that means taking fewer photos of yourself and more photos of what inspires you.

Take a minute to reflect on those hidden moments throughout your day and see what God is teaching you through them. Thank God for the opportunity you have to love and inspire people through social media, and ask for his wisdom to use it for his purpose. Ask him to draw you closer to him in your private and public lives.

16

Keep Your Focus

For whoever wants to save their life will lose it, but whoever loses their life for me and for the gospel will save it. What good is it for someone to gain the whole world, yet forfeit their soul?

MARK 8:35-36

When I was a teenager, I started thinking that if I worked hard, I could be successful as a basketball player. I gave all my time and attention to basketball. I daydreamed about making it big, going pro, and impressing people with my skills. I wanted to be a good steward of the gift God gave me. Wanting to excel in life is a really good thing. But when success and recognition become our obsession, we risk losing sight of what's actually important.

In the book of Daniel, we learn that Jerusalem was attacked and besieged by the king of Babylon. The

When success and recognition become our obsession, we risk losing sight of what's actually important.

Babylonians wanted to build the greatest empire in the world. They wanted to have the best, brightest, smartest kingdom of that time, so as they expanded their empire, they took the finest of Jerusalem's men and women back to Babylon. Daniel was one of those people.

The Babylonians knew that these dislocated people weren't just going to go with the flow and serve the kingdom after their people had been killed, their cities ransacked, and their culture destroyed. So they treated them well and gave them everything you could imagine for a life of luxury and success. They set them up to live in a palace, giving them the same delicious food that the king ate and access to the greatest, most sophisticated literature of that age.

Despite this, Daniel didn't lose sight of what was really important. He didn't give up his faith in God. He even refused to eat the king's food because it included meats God had told the Jews to avoid. Because Daniel stayed faithful, God blessed him as he grew older. Daniel was able to help the king several times and he saved many lives. Soon, the king promoted Daniel to a high position with a lot of power and responsibility and gave him great gifts, wealth, and fame. Still, Daniel remained focused on following God, praying, and spending time with him every day. Daniel understood something that the Babylonians didn't; he knew that all worldly success is nothing compared to life with God.

What about you? Where is your focus?

It's so easy to get caught up with climbing the ladder of success. I know this struggle personally because I face it every day. We can easily get sucked into the lie that we will be happier if we are more popular, if we have more social media followers, if we are perfect students, if we are the best athletes, if we make our bodies look better.

> All worldly success is nothing compared to life with God.

We should always strive to be the best that we can. But when we obsess over our social status and our idea of success, when we give more attention to these worldly things than we give to God, we put ourselves in danger of losing everything that makes our life worth living— faith, hope, and love. The good news is, keeping your focus on God isn't as hard as you might expect it to be. The key is reminding yourself of what's important by spending regular time with God. Pray every day, like Daniel, and ask God to keep you focused on following him. He will help and guide you.

Another key to keeping your focus is looking for ways you can help others. By wanting the best for some-one else, instead of for yourself, you turn your selfishness into love. Our natural inclination is to think about our-selves constantly. But fixating on ourselves so much is unhealthy. Taking the focus off ourselves and helping someone else reminds us of what's truly important: fol-lowing God and serving others. Pray for others, and help them whenever you can. George Washington Carver

By wanting the best for someone else, instead of for yourself, you turn your selfishness into love.

once said, "It is not the style of clothes one wears, neither the kind of automobile one drives, nor the amount of money one has in the bank, that counts. These mean nothing. It is simply service that measures success."

Today's world is a lot like old Babylon. It wants you to become comfortable and lose focus. It promises you more happiness if you keep running after success, whether that is in how many friends you have or how many points you score. But when we give all our attention and love to the world's idea of success, we don't have anything left for God. And when the world fails us, which it will, we'll truly be lost. Like with Daniel, if you keep your focus on following God, God will do great things in your life.

PRACTICE

Ask God to protect you from distractions that pull you away from following him, and pray for help to keep you focused on what is really important. Like Daniel when he refused to eat the meat from the king's table in order to obey God, take a minute or two to consider whether you need to make a change to keep your faith on track. Do you need to give up a bad habit or start a good habit?

Now shift your focus from yourself to others. Think about one or two people in your life and pray that God would bless them. Consider if there is a gift you can give or a service you can do for them to brighten their day. No matter if it's a big thing or a little gesture, make a plan to do it soon. By doing so, you will redirect your focus from selfish things to growing your relationship with Christ, which will last forever.

17

Word Power

The words of the mouth are deep waters, but the fountain of wisdom is a rushing stream.

PROVERBS 18:4

When I was younger, one of my high school coaches often told me that I thought too highly of myself and that I wasn't a good enough athlete. I had trained incredibly hard to be the best basketball player I could be, so to hear my coach tell me I wasn't good enough was really difficult. Because of his negative words, I second-guessed my skill, my playing style, even my desire to play the game in the first place. I lost confidence in myself and became afraid to play full out. Those words cut like a knife, and it took years to shake them off.

I'm sure you remember a time when someone's words hit you hard. Harmful words leave scars on our souls that don't easily heal. The old saying "sticks and stones may break my bones but words will never hurt me" is garbage. Whether we are aware of it or not, our words have a major effect on those around us.

Proverbs 18:21 says, "The tongue has the power of life and death, and those who love it will eat its fruit." I'm saddened to think about how many people struggle with depression, anxiety, eating disorders, or thoughts of suicide because of the thoughtless and malicious words of others. When we speak harm to anyone, we give them a taste of death. We have the power to speak life into the lives of others. With the words we say, we can heal wounds. And by speaking truth and comfort, we can save lives.

> ## When we speak harm to anyone, we give them a taste of death.

I am grateful to my college coach, Coach Barsh, who understood the power of words. In contrast to my high school coach, Barsh spoke words of encouragement and empowerment to me on and off the court. His words helped me heal from the harsh things others had said. Still, I fight the impact of negative words every day. For years, I've saved letters from my parents and close family friends in an old manila envelope. At times when I'm full of self-doubt and depression, or when I've lost sight of who I am as a child of God, I turn to those words of encouragement. That envelope is one of my most valued possessions because of the power of life-giving words.

As an athlete and now as a model, I meet and work with numerous people. But since I'm a quieter person, I do not like to talk as much as I like to sit back and observe, and by doing so, I've noticed how hurtful words can tear a person down, and how positive words can empower them. You can immediately see the effect on their face. It's reflected in their eyes. Shoulders sag when someone is hit with a negative word. But people stand up straighter, and their eyes brighten, when they're given an empowering word.

Words are contagious. If I speak a harsh word to a friend, they might respond with a harsh word in return, and the pattern repeats and repeats. My high school coach's words made me feel terrible, and when I feel down, I'm much more apt to say something cutting to another person. But if I lift someone up with my words, give some helpful advice, make them laugh, or give them a compliment, they're more willing to pass on the good vibes.

In the same way that words have a powerful effect on others, the words you say in your mind have a powerful effect on yourself. My dad used to tell me stories about his younger days as a college football player. During games, he made sure to keep his thoughts positive and to think words of encouragement. He didn't get down on himself after losses and instead kept his focus on always striving to do his best. It's so easy to be hard on ourselves when we mess up or when we don't do as well as we had hoped. I catch my thoughts repeating bad mantras to myself like, "You're so stupid," "Why did you have to go and mess that up?" or, "You're a bad person." But speaking negativity over ourselves never helps. It usually just makes the situation worse. And remember how words are contagious? If we speak terrible words to ourselves, the negativity will spill out of our mouths and onto others.

Instead of beating ourselves up, we can give more care to what words we use in our self-talk. If a negative mantra starts to pop into your mind the next time you mess up, try replacing it with something helpful or encouraging. For example, if you said something hurtful to a friend or sibling, don't tell yourself how bad you are. Instead, say something like, "Oops, that wasn't kind. But you got this—try again." Don't berate yourself if you messed up on an exam; say something like, "I will study more next time. I know I can do better."

Our thoughts are our most powerful coach. You can be a bad coach and use words to cut yourself down, or you can be a good coach who uses words as a resource to make yourself better. You'll be surprised by how well you'll do and how good you'll feel about yourself when you speak hope and encouragement into your own life.

The words we say are powerful, but the words of God are more powerful still.

Most importantly, remember that what matters most is what God says about you. So even if someone in your life continues to throw hurtful words at you, you don't have to believe them. The words we say are powerful, but the words of God are more powerful still. God calls you his child and his friend. He says he loves you and that he has your back. Every day, he is speaking words of love, joy, and hope over your life.

REFLECT

Think about what words you say to yourself. Do you speak helpful words to yourself or negative mantras? What about to others? Do you speak life or death to your friends and family? If you've been struggling to keep your words positive lately, don't berate yourself. Resolve to encourage yourself and others to do better.

Start saving the encouraging words people say about you in an envelope or write them in a notebook. When you're low or unsure of yourself, these words will help remind you of your identity as a child of God. Pray and ask God to teach you how to use the power of words well, to speak his truth, and love with yourself and those around you.

18

Persistent Obedience

Love the LORD your God with all
your heart and with all your soul
and with all your strength. These
commandments that I give you
today are to be on your hearts.

DEUTERONOMY 6:5-6

The word *obedience* gets some bad rap. Nobody likes
talking about rules and regulations. But if you take
Jesus seriously, you have to take the commands he gave
seriously. Jesus told his disciples, "If you love me, keep
my commands" (John 14:15).

If you only obey God when you feel like it, or when
you like the rules, then being a Christian is just a hobby
for you. Following Jesus takes consistent obedience. We
are commanded to do what God tells us to do. If we
know what we should do, but we don't do it, that's sin.
That may sound a little crazy, or even a little strict, but
that's what it means to give your life to God. If you love

God, and you want to follow Jesus, then you have to give it your all.

And honestly, this shouldn't surprise us. If I claim to be an athlete, but I never work out or practice, if I don't ever play the game, then everyone will call my bluff. If we claim to believe that Jesus is our God but we don't do what he says, then we are liars. Actions prove our beliefs.

Actions prove our beliefs.

Jesus was the only one who lived a life of perfect obedience to his Father. The Bible tells us that Jesus, just like any other human, was faced with every kind of temptation that we experience. But despite the temptations, he always chose to do the right thing. Perhaps the hardest moment of obedience for Jesus was the night before he was arrested and condemned to death. Jesus didn't want to die. He stayed up the whole night, wide awake and terrified because he knew the horrible things he was about to face. He prayed, "Father, if you are willing, take this cup from me; yet not my will, but yours be done" (Luke 22:42). Jesus knew that he could escape; he could run away from death on the cross. But that would mean rejecting God's call—it would mean disobedience. For Jesus, the cost of obeying God was his very life.

For Jesus and so many other biblical heroes, the cost of obedience was high. God didn't tell them how everything would work out in the end. He simply gave them a command and asked them to trust in him as their God. Look at Noah. God told Noah to build an ark in a desert where it rarely rained. The boat was so big that it took Noah and his three sons years to complete. All those years, Noah's neighbors ridiculed and made fun of him and his family. They were convinced Noah had lost his mind. But despite the public humiliation, Noah did what God told him to do. God asks the same of us today. He has probably not called you to build a ginormous boat in the desert, but perhaps he's given you a dream to work toward, no matter how long it takes or how ridiculous it looks to others. God asks each of us to give everything to him, our most prized and valuable things, our reputations. Following Jesus means giving our lives to him, no matter how hard it is.

This is a tough message, isn't it? Even Peter questioned Jesus about this, saying, "We have left everything to follow you! What then will there be for us?" And Jesus said to him, "Everyone who has left houses or brothers or sisters or father or mother or wife or children or fields for my sake will receive a hundred times as much and will inherit eternal life," (Matthew 19:27, 29). Remember: God is not cruel. Whether we see it or not, he always has a good purpose for every command and every task he gives us. And when we give him our lives, he honors our obedience by giving back in more wonderful ways than we can think, plus he gives us the gift of eternal life.

God doesn't waste any act of obedience. Though Noah suffered humiliation, his obedience saved his entire family and preserved life during the flood. And every believer who asks is forgiven through Jesus' obedience on the cross. Because of Jesus, every follower of Christ can experience the incredible love of God. God honors our obedience and works everything together according to his grand plan.

For us today, obedience is being faithful and following Jesus every day. It's not always easy or fun. Even though we may feel like God's commands are strange or hard to live out, we are called to trust him as our God. Obedience is doing what Jesus has told us to do in the Bible—praying, being with him day after day, and loving others as he loves us. And God will honor our obedience and use it to point others to Jesus.

REFLECT

Jesus explains what a life of obedience looks like in the book of Matthew, especially chapters 5-7. If you've never read this part of the Bible before, read it now. Then, for a few quiet moments, consider all the areas of your life—your life in school, church, work, sports, and everything else. Do you live fully obedient to God? When is it the hardest to obey God?

Pray in your mind or write in your journal, asking God to give you courage and faithfulness to obey him every day, all day long. Then ask God to give you wisdom and focus to follow Jesus.

19

Defender

Do not be overcome by evil, but overcome evil with good.

ROMANS 12:21

I transferred to a new school as my sophomore year of college began. Before I stepped foot on campus, people knew my name and that I was the new guy on the basketball team. One of my new teammates was not a fan of the attention I received on campus, especially from girls. He spread a nasty rumor to different girls around campus.

The rumor was so nasty that I started getting disgusted looks from all the students. I finally asked a female friend of mine, "What have I done to make everyone so upset with me?" She told me about the rumor. I was furious, to say the least, but I laughed it off. I knew that the rumor was untrue and that it had more to do with my teammate's personal issues than it had to do with me. My parents always taught me, "Do not repay evil with evil." So even though what my teammate did was foul and disrespectful, I let it go and forgave him.

If I had chosen to get even with my teammate and spread another rumor about him, you know what would have happened? I think I would have harmed myself further. I think all my teammates and everyone else on campus would have thought the first rumor was true, based on my bad response. I'm grateful that God gave me the ability to forgive him despite my initial anger. As soon as people got to know me, they knew the rumor was a lie. And soon the rumor disappeared altogether.

As you grow up, it is inevitable that people will let you down, betray, or hurt you. And we will all wrong someone else at some point. Someone may hurt you intentionally like my teammate, or simply by accident. And sometimes what we meant for good gets twisted and ends up hurting someone else. We can't always control what happens, but it's how we respond when we've been wronged that's important. When we are hurt or betrayed, we might become angry or want to get even. Our instinct will be to protect ourselves. But if you lash out, you will end up hurt-

Getting even doesn't bring about any justice at all.

ing yourself more than anyone else. Getting even doesn't bring about any justice at all. It only ends up keeping old wounds open.

Jesus tells us to resist our instincts and do the opposite. "But I tell you, love your enemies and pray for those who persecute you, that you may be children of your Father in heaven," he says (Matthew 5:44–45).

We cannot control the actions of other people. But we are still responsible for our own actions. If we get even, returning evil for evil, we are no better than those who betrayed us. But if we forgive and try to love those who hurt us, we end the pattern of evil. We can think of ourselves as partners with God in bringing peace and good back into the world.

Does this mean we just sit back and let people get away with terrible things? No, not at all. Galatians 6:7 says, "Do not be deceived: God cannot be mocked. A man reaps what he sows." God knows all things, and he doesn't let injustice stand. If any one of us hurts another, we will have to pay the consequences. And the same goes for anyone who does us wrong. We may not see what consequence they must pay, but we know that God is just. God is our judge and our protector. He is the one who deals out punishments and rewards, not us. He knows all things and understands more than we do, so we can trust that he will bring fairness and peace to every situation. Which means that when you experience betrayal or pain because of someone else's actions, you don't need to worry about getting even. God already has it handled, and he will defend you better than you can defend yourself.

Let go of your desire to get even and, instead, forgive those who do you harm.

Let go of your desire to get even and, instead, forgive those who do you harm. Pray for them, that they will come to know God's peace. Because that is what Jesus did for us. While we were sinners, rejecting his patient love, God did not lash out and destroy us. Instead, he sent his only Son to pay the consequence for our wrongs. And through that act of love, we are now able to forgive others just as he forgives us.

WRITE

Write down this verse as a reminder: "For if you forgive other people when they sin against you, your heavenly Father will also forgive you. But if you do not forgive others their sins, your Father will not forgive your sins" (Matthew 6:14–15).

As you journal, ask yourself if there is anyone that you need to forgive. Have you hurt someone and need to ask for their forgiveness? If there is something you need to do, whether it is talking to the person who caused you harm or asking someone for forgiveness, make a plan to do it as soon as possible. Pray that God will help you and give you the strength to forgive and ask for forgiveness.

20

Failure

Being confident of this, that he who began a good work in you will carry it on to completion until the day of Christ Jesus.

PHILIPPIANS 1:6

There is a confusing assumption that as soon as you make the decision to follow Jesus, everything becomes easier. We expect to become better people overnight, suddenly knowing all there is to know about living for God. But the opposite is more likely.

It's only when we start to live with integrity, trying to do the right things, that we realize how deep our sin goes. It's only when we begin resisting temptations that we'll really experience how powerful they are and how weak and sinful we really are. Maybe you feel the guilt of going a few days without spending time with God, or you angrily lashed out at someone, or maybe you're struggling with depression, despair, addictions, or deep wounds that only God can give words to. And no matter how hard you try, you just don't feel like you're making progress anymore.

What do we do when it seems like we're failing to follow Jesus?

When we experience setbacks or slow growth, we worry that we're just not made for this, that being a Christian is too hard, or that something is terribly wrong with us. We become disheartened and give up. But I want you to understand something: God loves the journey. He doesn't hyper-jump you to the final destination the moment

God loves the journey.

you give your life to him. God is a storyteller and he loves the process, the seasons, and daily minute-by-minute choices to follow him.

Remember Moses? God appeared to him in a burning bush and called him to lead the Israelites out of slavery. Moses had lots of excuses for why he wasn't the right guy for the job, but in the end, he obeyed God. And God did many powerful miracles through Moses to rescue his people. But once they were free, Moses and the Israelites found themselves in the desert—without food, water, or a home. For forty years, God instructed Moses to lead the Israelites in that desert. They traveled from place to place, set up camp for a few days, and then moved on. And each day, God miraculously provided water and food for all the people. As you can imagine, the people grew tired easily, and they complained often. They had thought freedom meant an easier life than slavery, not a life of living hand-to-mouth in the wilderness. They felt lost and discouraged. But God wasn't only focused on getting his people through the desert. He was interested in the journey their souls were taking.

In the wilderness, God taught them how to wait for his timing every day, how to follow where he led, and to trust that he would provide everything they needed. There were many setbacks along the way, but God used each one to show Moses and the Israelites his jus-

> We all have a God-designed plan that will lead us, step by patient step, toward him.

tice, mercy, forgiveness, and power. And as a result, the story of the Israelites in the wilderness continues to be a reminder for all of us of God's provision and faithfulness. The Israelites' physical journey seemed aimless, but every step of their spiritual journey was bringing them closer and closer to God. We all have a God-designed plan that will lead us, step by patient step, toward him.

What do we do when we don't see any progress? We keep walking, step by step. Be faithful with what you already know to do, like spending time with God each day, following his commands, praying, and reading Scripture. Meet with your mentor if you can and ask their advice on ways to keep growing. Hang with friends who are growing in their faith so that you can encourage each other. Try to help someone else in their journey. Taking your focus off yourself and then serving others can give you a new perspective on your own journey.

We will fail. We will slip up. We shouldn't seek to stumble or become callous to our failures, because our aim is the holiness of a gracious and just God. But we also do not need to be overly upset about our setbacks. Satan wants you to panic when you don't see progress. He wants you to become discouraged and give up. But God never discourages his people. Instead, Jesus calls you to step closer to him, to share each struggle with him so that he can help you conquer it.

Even though we may feel like we're failing, God never fails. God uses both days of growth and days of wandering for your good and for his glory. He always keeps his promises, and he will never stop working in you to help you grow into the person he created you to be. So don't become disheartened when you're not seeing the results you hoped for. Instead, keep pursuing Christ, trusting that he is continuing the good work he has begun in you.

REFLECT

Think about your spiritual journey over the last years. Where did you start out? Where are you now, and what were the major milestones that brought you here? What kind of journey are you on now, and what do you think you are learning?

Reflecting on your spiritual journey can be an encouragement as you glimpse the big picture of God's plan in your life. Write a prayer thanking God for bringing you closer to him, step by step.

21

Give Thanks

So then, just as you received Christ Jesus as Lord, continue to live your lives in him, rooted and built up in him, strengthened in the faith as you were taught, and overflowing with thankfulness.

COLOSSIANS 2:6–7

We've talked about keeping your head up when you're discouraged about your spiritual growth. We've talked about how to keep your focus when you feel like you're wandering, lost in the wilderness like Moses and the Israelites. One of the best ways to keep strong is by practicing thankfulness.

Thankfulness can seem powerless when you're struggling academically, when there are more bills than money left at the end of the month, when you have been obedient to God in keeping yourself pure but your innocence was stolen anyway, or when your family is being torn apart. In the face of these awful situations, being thankful sounds like a cheap way to make light of our pain. It seems like a cop-out, you might think. But practiced thankfulness is one of the most overlooked and most powerful tools at your disposal. It's not simply a Band-Aid for our brokenness; it works like a salve for our wounds.

> But practiced thankfulness is one of the most overlooked and most powerful tools at your disposal.

First, thankfulness reminds us of God's goodness. When we are going through tough times, we focus on all that is going wrong and we forget what is going right. Even when life is going pretty well for us, we easily become immune to the gifts we experience every day—like the companionship of friends and family, education, water, food, even the greater gifts of knowing God, salvation, and the hope that one day all things will be put right. Being thankful helps us to notice all the gifts God gives us every day.

Gratefulness shifts our perspective from our own little world to God's grand plan. When we remember to be grateful for the good things, we are able to withstand more disappointments and struggles. And because we know that nothing can ruin God's plan for us, we can even give thanks for the bad things in life. The disciple Peter wrote about this to Christians who were being persecuted for their faith. He told them that hard times come so that their faith, which is even more valuable than our life on earth, has the opportunity to grow. Like a muscle, if our faith is not tested and pushed to the limit, it will only become weak. But when our faith grows, God can use our lives for great things that bring him glory and honor, which shows the world his amazing love (1 Peter 1:6–7).

It's easy to be grateful when life is going well, when things are easy and the sun is shining. It is much harder to remain thankful when life is hard, when the worst things are coming true, when it seems the sun has been ripped out of the sky. So in the middle of these dark times, how do we practice thankfulness?

Gratefulness is the opposite of complaining. Take care not to complain too much, in your mind or out loud. It's good and healthy to talk about your struggles with others and explain why you're feeling down. But if everything you think and say is a complaint, that's a clear sign that your focus isn't where it should be. There is no room for growth or hope in a heart that complains. Philippians 2:14–15 says, "Do everything without grumbling or arguing, so that you may become blameless and pure, 'children of God without fault' . . ."

There is no room for growth or hope in a heart that complains.

When you find your mind centering on negative thoughts, try to shift it a little by finding one thing to be grateful for.

If you want to know if you're living a life of thankfulness, listen to your own prayers. An attitude of entitlement will give God a list of requests. But an attitude of gratefulness will praise God for his gifts and intercede for the needs of others.

Whatever situation you find yourself in, no matter if it's good or bad, you can choose to practice gratitude, knowing that God is faithful and working in you. He is with you, caring and providing for you in more ways than you can know.

PRACTICE

Consider your thoughts, the words you say, and your prayers. Do you tend to complain? Shift your perspective by practicing thankfulness. In your journal, make a list of things you are grateful for. Try to fill the page. Then pray and thank God for two or three things from your list. Thank him for giving you eternal life and a purpose. Ask him to open your eyes to see his gifts wherever you are, and whatever situation you're in.

22

Take Notice

For it is God who works in you to will and to act in order to fulfill his good purpose.

PHILIPPIANS 2:13

Have you ever felt that God moves in the lives of others more than in your own? Many of us struggle with the fear that God doesn't actually act in our lives, that we are somehow excluded from seeing him work. That's especially true today, as it seems everything is visible through social media and technology. We watch religious leaders like famous pastors, Christian athletes, and Christian artists who post like they see God almost constantly working in their lives. I know I look at my own life and fear that I am somehow cut off from seeing God move and act. But this fear is a lie. And to beat it, we must confront it in two ways.

First, we have to tackle the worst part of the lie. It's the part that convinces us we don't see God move in our lives because God doesn't love us as much as others, that he doesn't care as much about us as he does his other children, and that we're somehow less than everyone else. Satan uses this lie often because it is so crippling. It steals our confidence in our holy Father and our confidence in our identity as a child of God. With this tactic, we become trapped in a cycle of comparing our lives to the idea of what we think someone else's life must be like—even though we don't really know what they are experiencing. And the cycle distracts our focus from spending time with God.

When I feel myself slipping into believing this lie, I reflect on verses like Acts 10:34–35, which says that God shows no favoritism but accepts all who follow and obey him, and Isaiah 43:10, which says, "'You are my witnesses,' declares the LORD, 'and my servant whom I have chosen, so that you may know and believe me and understand that I am he.'" No matter what we fear or what lies we face, God has told us that he has specifically chosen each one of us. We are not loved or cared for less than anyone else. And we have proof in the life, death, and resurrection of Jesus Christ. God is bigger than we think he is, and more compassionate than we can imagine—with exuberant energy spent every day on you in particular. He has immense interest in each detail about your life. He is already moving and speaking to you. But you have to open your eyes to notice all that he is doing.

That is the second level of defense against this lie: learning to notice and appreciate God's daily actions. Thinking God isn't doing anything in your life, that he's not working in and around you, is simply not true. And believing this lie causes you to miss out on all the things he's doing right now, right here. When we stop and think on God's daily gifts, we start to see him work. We begin noticing his blessings, like the gifts of life, breath, and health. God cares for his followers, even in very small ways. Do you remember the Israelites and how God led them in the wilderness for years? Deuteronomy 29:2–6 describes how God provided food and water for them and protected their clothing and shoes from wearing out. He cares about his children so much that he even thinks about the state of their shoes.

> When we stop and think on God's daily gifts, we start to see him work.

One of my favorite examples of God's care features a prophet in the Bible, Elijah. Elijah followed and obeyed God faithfully, and because of that, God used him to do some amazing miracles. But after many years, Elijah was exhausted physically, emotionally, and spiritually. 1 Kings 19 tells how Elijah, exhausted as he was, laid down under a tree and slept. He half expected to die, but God woke him up and gave him bread to eat. And the bread was divine food that gave strength for Elijah's body, heart, and soul.

In the same way, God provides for each of us in ways that strengthen every area of our selves. We just have to tune in and recognize it. Pay attention when someone gives you an encouraging word or a piece of advice, because that may be God giving you strength and help. Appreciate the love of your family and the companionship you have with friends, because that too is a gift from God. Food, shelter, music, art, laughter, community . . . all these things are signs of God's love for you.

When these gifts, no matter how big or small, no longer mean anything to us, that's when we know we have become blind to God's actions.

Noticing these little things—like food, family, and shelter—helps us to be aware of the bigger works of God. I can't tell you how many times I've wrestled with a question about faith, and the very next Sunday, the pastor will speak about that exact topic. That's God's timing. Every answer to prayer is a testament to God moving in and around us.

When these gifts, no matter how big or small, no longer mean anything to us, that's when we know we have become blind to God's actions. We have taken his blessings for granted and become so used to them that we don't even see them anymore.

So how do we defend against this lie that God isn't moving in our lives? First, remind yourself of God's amazing love for you and that he chooses no favorites. He can move and speak in your life just as much as he moves and speaks in everyone else's. And second, be on the lookout and pay attention to your life. God is moving even right here, right now. Open your eyes and take notice.

WRITE

Try to think about your life in terms of how God has moved in and around you. Reflect on a time when you helped someone else and how God was there giving you the right words to say or the wisdom to know the right thing to do. Think about a time when someone said or did something that meant a lot to you. Journal about a few of these important moments in your life, thanking God for being active in and around you. Thank him for the little blessings that keep you strengthened. And ask him to open your eyes to see his work more and more.

23

Are You Weak Enough?

My grace is all you need. My power
works best in weakness.

2 CORINTHIANS 12:9 (NLT)

Our world values strength and power above all else.
At an early age, we are all trained to work hard
to be strong, capable, without any flaws. Weakness is
always bad, weakness is always a problem . . . right?

One day, Jesus and his disciples passed a man who
was born blind. In that time and culture, people who
lived with any kind of disability were looked down on.
Any sign of weakness was thought to be a punishment
from God for some sin they had committed. And sadly,
they were often isolated and pushed out of society by
their own peers. Thinking about all this, the disciples
asked Jesus, "Who sinned, this man or his parents, that
he was born blind?"

And Jesus surprised them by saying, "Neither this man nor his parents sinned, but this happened so that the works of God might be displayed in him" (John 9:2–3). Then Jesus healed the man and restored his sight.

Word spread about Jesus' miracle, and the religious leaders of that day—who were already jealous of Jesus—called the man into court to explain what happened. The man told them the whole story, and when they refused to believe that Jesus was the Son of God, he challenged their thinking. The leaders became so mad that they kicked the formerly blind man out of the temple; he could no longer go to the temple and worship God with his family.

Think about how this guy must have felt. He had been born blind and rejected by society, then he was miraculously, unbelievably healed. But still, he was kicked out and denied the chance to worship the one who had healed him. He must have felt so confused and hurt. But Jesus found him again, and after they talked, the man became a follower of Christ. Though everyone thought this man was cursed and weak, God used him to show his power. He was not only physically healed but also spiritually healed as he came face to face with Jesus and experienced his love. At last he was accepted— accepted into God's family.

On top of all that, God used this man to speak truth to the religious leaders, to challenge their stubbornness, and give them another opportunity to experience that same spiritual healing. The Bible doesn't give this man's name, but through his story, many people—from the disciples then, to you and me today—are encouraged and inspired by God's healing and love. It wasn't *in spite of* this man's blindness that God worked through him, it was *because of* his weakness that God used his life to show his power.

When I think about this story, I have to ask myself: Am I weak enough for God to use me? Do I let God use my faults for his glory, or do I try to hide them? Because of our society's obsession with strength, whenever we sense weakness in ourselves, we try to cover it up. But what if we looked for ways God uses our weakness to show his strength? The difficulties we experience now become part of our story. They help us, sometimes painfully, along the path toward the person God is creating each one of us to be. He allows us to experience the disabling things of life that cause us

What if we looked for ways God uses our weakness to show his strength?

deep pain to keep us humble and completely dependent on him.

I dreamed of playing ball after college, but couldn't because of chronic back pain. That injury, that *weakness*, completely altered the direction of my life. There was a time I thought my usefulness to God was gone because I wasn't strong in the way that I thought I should be. But now, I can see how God is using me and my weaknesses to bring me closer to him, and to help draw others to him as well.

Sometimes, God uses our weaknesses by healing them, like he healed the man's blindness. Other times, God uses a struggle to help us trust him and rely on his grace. Paul says, "Therefore I will boast all the more gladly about my weaknesses, so that Christ's power may rest on me" (2 Corinthians 12:9).

Our weaknesses, no matter what they are, are God's tools. Our weaknesses keep us humble, so that we rely on God's help and are willing to be used by God in whatever way he chooses. Like the blind man, our weaknesses bring glory to God because any victory, any success, is God's work alone. And like he did for me, God uses our weaknesses to redirect our lives according to his master plan, to show the world his love.

> **Our weaknesses, no matter what they are, are God's tools.**

We should always seek to grow and become better people, to conquer our faults. But when you think about your weaknesses, don't let despair grab hold of you. Trust God to use your weaknesses for good.

REFLECT

What are your weaknesses? How do you feel they hold you back from being the person you want to be? Now think about how God might be using them to help you become a better person. Think about how you can be an instrument of God's love to others through your weakness. Spend a few minutes in prayer. Talk to God about your weakness. You can be honest. You can tell him how hard it is to live with this struggle. Ask him to use your weakness for good and to strengthen your faith and the faith of those around you.

God Is Your Keeper

I am with you and will watch over
you wherever you go.
GENESIS 28:15

Thousands of years ago, an army marched against the small country of Judah. This army was massive, combining hundreds of soldiers from three other countries. The king of Judah, a man named Jehoshaphat, knew that his little kingdom stood no chance in this battle. An army that size could easily wipe out all of Jehoshaphat's soldiers and destroy his cities along with all the men, women, and children living in them.

So Jehoshaphat called all his people together to fast and to pray. No matter how far away they lived, everyone gathered at the temple. In front of the people, Jehoshaphat prayed and said to God, "You rule over all the kingdoms of the nations. Power and might are in your hand, and no one can withstand you." As he prayed, Jehoshaphat remembered all the things God did that made Judah the flourishing country that it had become. He ended his prayer by saying, "We do not know what to do, but our eyes are on you" (2 Chronicles 20:6, 12).

The king and all the people stood there, before the temple, and waited. Then God spoke through a prophet and told them not to be afraid. He instructed Jehoshaphat to take his men in the morning and march toward the army. God promised them that all they had to do was stand firm and that he would fight for them.

The next morning, Jehoshaphat followed God's orders and marched his men toward the army. And when they got there, they saw that the army had been destroyed. God had turned the different countries in the army against each other. Not one soldier from Judah had to lift a weapon.

I think I would have panicked if I was King Jehoshaphat. Faced with an army like that, one that was determined to wipe out everything in its path, it's amazing that Jehoshaphat didn't give up and run away. Instead, he remembered God's promises, he gathered the people before the Lord, and he sought help. And God, who promises to hear the prayers of his followers and who always has our backs, kept his promise and rescued his people. This story reminds me that no matter what we are up against, we can ask God for his help.

I'm grateful that I'm not faced with an invading army like Jehoshaphat, but I do deal with regular opposition just like you do. But by praying and following God, I've seen God come through for me in amazing ways. Remember the story about that awful rumor my teammate spread about me? That rumor dissolved into nothing. Some people don't like that I speak out about my faith, and they criticize me for it. Sometimes after asking for God's help, I get a new idea and realize how to respond to criticism. Other times, God points me toward a person who can help me solve a problem.

I've learned, like Jehoshaphat did, that whenever I come up against a challenge I don't think I can conquer, I can pass it to God and ask for his help.

Surprisingly, after I pray, I often realize God has already gone ahead of me to help, just like he went ahead of Jehoshaphat's men and destroyed the enemy for them.

After I pray, I often realize God has already gone ahead of me to help.

God wants to protect you and keep you. As Psalm 121 says, the maker of heaven and earth is our help and he is always vigilant to protect us.

The most inspiring thing to me about Jehoshaphat's story is that after he ended his prayer, he waited for God's response. In our haste to see our problems solved, we usually don't stick around long enough to hear what God has to say to us. But the people of Judah *expected* God to speak to them. We have to remember that God not only wants to help us, he also wants to speak to us. When we are first learning to listen to God, it takes patience. And sometimes God speaks through the words of other people, as he spoke through the prophet. But he does speak if we are careful to listen.

You might be facing your own kind of army right now. Maybe you're dealing with depression or agonizing

In our haste to see our problems solved, we usually don't stick around long enough to hear what God has to say to us.

thoughts. You might be struggling against a bully or peer pressure. Your family may be fighting each other, or maybe you are fighting yourself in some way. But no matter what you are up against, God says, "Be strong and courageous. Do not be afraid; do not be discouraged, for the LORD your God will be with you wherever you go" (Joshua 1:9).

God is your keeper. If you're up against a tough situation, ask God for his help and listen carefully for his words to you. And then watch and see how God is already at work in your life.

I hope it is a comfort to you to know that you are never alone, that God always has your back. He's there for you when you need someone to talk to. If you ask, he will give you peace and wisdom, and he will help you deal with every obstacle. And when tough situations are thrown at you, you can trust that God is already in the middle of it, working things out for the good.

God will come through for you!

PRACTICE

What is the army you're facing right now? It might be an annoying obstacle, or maybe you're not sure how to solve a certain problem. Or it might be a terribly difficult thing to deal with. No matter what it is, pray and ask God for his help. Tell him about what you are struggling with and then try listening for his words to you. He might speak to you with an idea on how to fix your problem, or remind you of his promise to be with you, no matter what. If you don't feel like he's speaking to you, don't worry. Go about your day, and try to watch and listen to how God is speaking and helping you. Some problems take a few days of consistent prayer before you see any change, some problems take years. But don't give up—keep praying, keep listening, keep watching.

25

When Plans Fall Apart

In their hearts humans plan their course, but the Lord establishes their steps.

PROVERBS 16:9

I always have a plan. As I roll out of bed and my feet hit the floor, I know what I have to do that day. I have a mental schedule and a checklist of the tasks I want to complete. I've always been this way, and I think it goes back to my basketball days. As some of you know, when you are involved in an intense sport, team, or club, it takes up a lot of your time. You need to have a plan in order to know what to do and when to do it.

But we don't just plan our days—we plan our lives. Especially in our culture, we are encouraged from our early years to have a plan for the future. How many times have you been asked what you want to do when you grow up? What major you want to pursue in college? What your dream job is? All these questions drive at our inclination to make plans. But plans don't always work out.

If you had asked what my plans were when I was in high school, I would have responded pretty confidently that I was going to be a pro basketball player. All through high school and into college, I was making that dream come true. Then one winter, all those plans were ruined.

Within just weeks of each other, I injured my knee and my dad was diagnosed with cancer. My knee injury was so bad, I needed surgery. Doctors told me my basketball career was over. At the same time, I watched as my dad fought for his life, dealing with symptoms of the terrible disease and all the side effects of chemotherapy. My future, which had seemed so clear, was now gone. I didn't know who I was anymore, or what I was going to do with my life.

My future, which had seemed so clear, was now gone.

In the Bible, we find a young kid named Joseph. I think that Joseph was probably similar to me when I was younger, thinking he knew what his future would be like. I imagine his plans were pretty clear. Joseph probably figured he would follow in his father's steps and take over the management of his family's flocks and herds. One day he would marry and have children of his own. When his father died, he would inherit more money and animals. He would be a wealthy man, like his dad. Things looked pretty good to him.

But that's not how Joseph's future turned out. His plans hardly had a chance to come into his imagination before his brothers, jealous of him being the favorite, sold him to slavers who brought him to Egypt, where Joseph became a servant in an Egyptian noble's house.

It couldn't have been easy, that transition from a free man, someone favored in his home, to the bottom of the barrel in a foreign land. Egyptians spoke a different language, they worshiped other gods, and they had a totally different set of values than what Joseph had been raised with. But over time, Joseph adapted his plans. He set his mind to do the best he could wherever he was. God blessed his work, and Joseph became head of the noble's household, trusted with everything his master owned.

But then, Joseph's plans fell apart again, and he was thrown into prison for a crime he didn't commit. You would think Joseph would have just given up at that point. But he adapted again and learned how to do his best even in jail. It wasn't long before the warden noticed how trustworthy and hardworking Joseph was. He gave him responsibilities to help manage the prison.

Like Joseph, I tried to adapt my plans and do the best I could where I was. I committed to praying every day for my dad to make a full recovery. I went to physical therapy and worked hard to strengthen my knee. And thanks to God's grace, my dad beat cancer! After a few long months, I was back on the court. But my plans are not what they used to be. Because of that tough winter and God's work in my life, I realized I wasn't meant to be a professional basketball player. Though I love the sport, God has called me to help others in a different way— through speaking and writing, through my relationships with friends and family, and through being a good role model.

Our plans rarely turn out the way we think they will. As you talk to parents and mentors in your life, you'll start to notice that not many people are where they dreamed they would be when they were younger. It took me a while to learn that there is not a perfect path from high school to college to career. Plans don't always work out. God leads everyone on their own journey, and no two journeys are alike.

As you grow, I hope you still make plans and dream big dreams. Goals give your life direction and momentum. Without plans, we would all just wander through our days. That's not a good use of the one amazing life God has given each of us. But you have to be ready to know how to respond when things don't turn out the way you think they will.

Here's the key: hold your plans in an open hand. By that, I mean don't hold on to your plans so tightly that, if they fall apart like they did for me, you lose your identity. The book of James warns

As you dream, remember to hold your plans loosely and allow God to direct your journey.

against holding too tightly to our expectations: "Instead, you ought to say, 'If it is the Lord's will, we will live and do this or that'" (James 4:15). After all, we can't predict the future. As you dream, remember to hold your plans loosely and allow God to direct your journey.

When life does fall apart, my prayer for you is that

you'll press closer to God like never before. He gets it. He knows the sorrow and the frustration that comes with ruined plans. And like a perfect father, he is there for you. When you're ready, take a look around and see how you can be the best you can be right where you are. Like Joseph, if you work hard and seek to do your best even in the worst times, God will bless you.

Joseph, through a crazy turn of events, went from working in the prison to the ruler of all Egypt, second only to Pharaoh himself. Though God's plans are often not what we have in mind, his ways are always better than ours.

WRITE

What are your plans for the future? Write them down in your journal today. Where do you think you will be in five years? What about ten years? Do you think that this is the plan God has for you? Now spend a few minutes in prayer and imagine taking that journal page with all your plans and handing it to Jesus. Think about holding your dreams loosely, working to do the best you can with the life you've been given while still being open to God's design. At the top of the page, write "God willing" as a way to show your willingness to follow his plans.

If you are in that place where you feel all your plans have fallen apart and you are dealing with a really tough situation right now, I encourage you to read the story of Joseph in Genesis 37–45. Notice how God is with him in every step of his journey. Take a moment today to reflect on the ways you can be the best you can be even in the middle of this situation. Pray and ask God for his protection and guidance to know what to do.

26

The Good and the Bad

The righteous person may have many troubles, but the LORD delivers him from them all.

PSALM 34:19

I f you lived for many years following God as best you could, but life turned out terrible for you anyway, would you keep following him? If you lost everything that was meaningful to you—relationships, possessions, skills, talents, health—would you still want to know God? If we're honest, I think a lot of us, me included, would have a hard time saying yes.

We often treat God like a machine that, with the right amount of prayer and Bible reading, grants us special wishes and easy lives. We assume that if we obey his commands and work to be generally good people, God will reward our behavior by giving us blessings and success. But this assumption leaves us empty when we are suddenly faced with terrible things like the loss of a parent, divorce in the family, illness, depression, or any number of other heart-wrenching scenarios. We are left with a question: Why do bad things happen to good people?

This is a tough subject to be sure, and we often don't like the answers. Bad stuff happens to bad people and also to good people, and no one knew this better than Job.

The book of Job tries to offer an explanation to this question. In this book we meet Job, a man who truly had it all. He was very wealthy and he had a large, healthy family. He had many animals to work in his fields and everything he needed for a life of luxury. The Bible describes him as the greatest man among all the people. Job understood that all these things were gifts from God, and he followed God faithfully. But in one day, everything he had was taken away. His children were killed, all his livestock was destroyed, his wealth was ruined. Even his health was taken by a painful sickness.

For the kind of deep pain Job experienced, there is no comfort. There are things in this life, sadly, that cut the heart. There are no words anyone can say that help that kind of dark sorrow. Sometimes there is no silver lining. I know what it's like to feel that kind of pain.

After my dad was diagnosed with cancer, I had to fly back to college. I went through knee surgery to repair the damage from my basketball injury. And then I broke up with the girl I thought I would marry. In a very short period of time, three big parts of my life changed forever, and I wasn't able to handle it all. I spiraled into a depression for several months after that. I kept slipping further and further until I was in such a dark place that I tried to take my own life. But God helped me survive. All night long, he sent images of my family flashing through my mind. If it weren't for that, I don't think I would be here today.

At times, I wanted to blame God. My dad didn't deserve cancer. He had followed God and served in ministry for years. I couldn't think of what I had done to deserve all these other bad things coming at me. Not many people understood my questions. But Job did.

Job grieved for his sons and daughters for seven days. Then he began processing his grief. He told his friends he wished he had never been born and listed all the ways he followed God. He asked God to explain why it all happened to him, a devout follower of God. And then God spoke to him. He reminded Job that he is God, he made the earth, he is master of justice and mercy. He cares for all of creation.

And God reminded Job that he didn't owe Job anything. Though God loves us all, we are his created. We don't get to make demands of him. If we were able to order God around, then he wouldn't be God after all. And if we only love him for what we hope to get out of the relationship, that's not love—that's manipulation. God wants us to love him freely, without strings attached. Though God never does anything evil, he uses the bad things in life to help us choose to follow him because we love him, not because we want something from him. When everything is stripped from us, we are

And if we only love him for what we hope to get out of the relationship, that's not love—that's manipulation.

left with what's in our heart. We decide if what's left is manipulation and selfishness, or love.

After God speaks, Job is amazed at God's power and wisdom. His trust in God's justice is confirmed. He says, "My ears had heard of you but now my eyes have seen you" (Job 42:5). Job loved God not just for what he gave him, but for who he is. The book ends with God giving back everything that Job lost. Job's livestock and his wealth is doubled. Job even has ten more children.

> Job loved God not just for what he gave him, but for who he is.

During the tough time in my life, it was helpful to notice that God let Job grieve. God, our creator, knows that grief is part of being human, and he listens to our complaints. He wants us to deal with our emotions in a healthy way.

It takes time to process emotions, so if you're going through something right now, remember to be patient with yourself. If you're angry, find a good outlet. If you're dealing with too many emotions to count, try journaling, drawing, or painting to help yourself process. After God protected me from that awful night, I read the Bible a lot to remind me of who God is and the promises he makes to his children. And I spent a lot of time with family and friends, patiently talking things out when I needed to and just being with others when I needed company.

If you are walking through your own dark night right now, try to talk to someone. I know it doesn't sound like it would be helpful, especially if you feel particularly depressed. But we humans were never made to walk alone. Talk to someone, such as a parent or older sibling, a teacher, mentor, your youth group leader, or a counselor.

God is with us, transforming the terrible things into good. And he offers each one of us his comforting and powerful presence. He reminds us that he alone is God. He holds it all in his hands; he is in control. All we have to do is love him for who he is.

REFLECT

What do you think you would do if you were Job? Have you lost something very important to you? Are you angry at God for something that you experienced? Do you feel like you deserve a different life? Take a few minutes and pray. You can be very honest with God. You can say, "God, this feels very unfair, and I don't understand any of it. But I know you are good, I know you are just. Please help me now. Work all these broken things together for good."

27

Repent

Those who have been born into God's family do not make a practice of sinning, because God's life is in them. So they can't keep on sinning, because they are children of God.

1 JOHN 3:9 (NLT)

Sin is like mold. It grows in the corners and behind the basement steps of our lives, places we don't see. And that is part of its danger. Sin works best if you don't notice it. The more you're unaware of it, the more it can grow unchecked.

As we grow in our faith and start following Jesus intentionally, it's tempting to think that we put this whole sin thing behind us. But that's not true. While we are on earth, we still have to resist sin. And we have to routinely clean all the little corners in our hearts to make sure sin isn't infecting our lives.

Sin coaxes us to do things that aren't good. It

encourages us to be angry, to disrespect and abuse others, to ignore God. You can see it everywhere, from the lie we whisper in our minds telling us we're not loved by God, to feeling envious of someone because they have what we don't, to speaking outright hatred toward another person. It makes us a prisoner, controlling our thoughts, emotions, and words. And the worst part is that we often don't even notice that it's there, silently controlling what we do and think and say.

Sin separates us from God, hindering the intimacy of our relationship. Paul tells the Ephesian Christians, "Do not grieve the Holy Spirit of God, with whom you were sealed for the day of redemption. Get rid of all bitterness, rage and anger, brawling and slander, along with every form of malice" (Ephesians 4:30–31). God has given us the power to live free of sin. When we become apathetic, letting sin fester inside, it makes God sad for us. Plus, if we let sin keep growing in our lives when we know better, do you think we can consider ourselves followers of Christ?

When you believe that Jesus is God, ask for his forgiveness, and decide to follow him, you are no longer trapped in sin. The thing that used to control us no longer has power over us; God's grace shows us the way to live clean, free lives. This is truly amazing! Through God's Word and through his commandments, we are taught how to recognize sin and we are given the ability to make our own choices, to decide our own thoughts. Because Jesus paid the price for our sins by dying in our place, we are now free of sin's power and control.

How do we make sure we're not slipping into sin

again? From the first book of the Bible to the last, God teaches us to notice if we're going in the wrong direction and to turn around. The early Christians called this process repentance. Repentance means realizing your mistakes; it means transitioning from walking the wrong way to walking down the right path. With each act of repentance, I'm a little freer from sin's power. Each course correction brings me closer to God. After repenting, all my sense of guilt and the feeling of not being good enough is gone. It's a beautiful, liberating feeling knowing that God is with me, helping me root out all sin and standing ready to forgive me the minute I ask.

> It's a beautiful, liberating feeling knowing that God is with me, helping me root out all sin and standing ready to forgive me the minute I ask.

Martin Luther, a historic church leader, said that all of our lives are an act of repentance. All of life is a constant turning back to God. Every day, I make mistakes. In college, I got too involved in the party scene with all the accompanying alcohol and drugs. I've had to learn how to live a life of sexual purity. I catch myself holding on to anger and bitterness when I should forgive. I lie to protect my reputation when I should be honest. I give more attention and priority to other things than to my relationship with God. I've had to learn the hard way to make it a habit to pause and reflect on my actions. I pray and ask God to check every corner of my heart and mind and show me any mold, any sin that's growing in my life. And when something comes to mind, I ask for God's forgiveness and ask his wisdom to know how to do better the next time.

A lot of us struggle to admit when we are wrong, or doing something less than perfect. That's how a lot of Christians have hurt other people—by lying to themselves and to others about their mistakes. We feel pressure, as people who claim to follow God, to be perfect. But obviously, that's not possible. And lying and putting on a false face is itself a sin. That means repentance is really the most authentic thing you can do. Repentance is about putting down the deception of who we think we are and coming to terms with who we really are, the good and the bad. It's admitting to God, honestly and openly, when you've screwed up and then purposefully returning to what is right and true.

In the middle of the day, when I feel like I've become distracted with all the things I have to do, or when I catch myself messing up, I pray the Jesus prayer in my mind. Jesus taught this short prayer to the disciples in Luke 18:13, and it goes like: Jesus Christ, son of the living God, have mercy on me, a sinner. No matter where I am or what I'm doing, I can pray this little prayer to re-center my mind and heart on Christ.

Just like spending regular time with God is a healthy habit, so is the practice of repentance. It corrects our path when we slip off course, it helps us to be self-aware, and it enables us to draw closer to God. It is a tool God uses to bring us closer to his holiness and love.

PRACTICE

If you haven't practiced repentance before, let's try it today. Like mold, sin is often difficult to detect on our own, so first pray and ask God to show you the sin in your life. Sit and listen for a few minutes, then think back over your last few days. Have you let anything get between you and your relationship with God? What actions are you least proud of? Did you say or do anything hurtful to someone else? Why did you do it/what pushed you to do it? Pray again, this time speaking very honestly to God about what you did and why. Don't make excuses. Say you are sorry, and ask for his forgiveness. End your prayer asking for the strength and the wisdom to do better next time.

It is good to be sorry, to feel the sorrow of disappointing God. But note that you don't need to feel awful about yourself because of your mistakes. Through repentance, God wants you to grow and to return to what is right. Don't drag yourself through the mud, so to speak, but rather focus on how to keep growing closer to God.

28

You Are Light

"Let your light shine before others,
that they may see your good deeds
and glorify your Father in heaven."
MATTHEW 5:16

People can be very hypocritical, can't they? I think it has something to do with our culture right now. To compete with the loud world out there, we feel pressured to say things without actually believing them or backing them up with our actions. How many of us say we are environmentally friendly but we don't recycle, or we claim to be politically informed but only listen to one news source? As Christians, we can't just give lip service at church, say a quick prayer for the day, and call it good. We have to back up our faith with

We have to back up our faith with actions. Otherwise, we are hypocrites.

actions. Otherwise, we are hypocrites. And we're not fooling anyone.

When I read the verse at the start of this devotion, I take it personally. I feel myself standing in the crowd Jesus was preaching to. I imagine his eyes meeting mine as he says, "You are the light of the world ... Let your light shine before others." I am intimidated because I know that the whole purpose of the light is to expel the darkness and to show others the way. The eyes of people around me—my wife, my son, my family, my friends, the people I work with, the people I bump into on the street, the barista who makes my coffee, the postman, the other drivers on the road—they're all watching me. And when people see me, they should see Christ.

When someone learns that I'm a Christian, the best compliment they can give is to say, "Yeah, I could tell." How sad would it be if, instead, they said, "Really? I didn't think you cared about that stuff."

After Jesus returned to heaven, Peter and John told everyone who would listen about their faith. And the same religious leaders who sentenced Jesus to death hated them. They felt that the disciples were ruining the purity of the Jewish faith, so they called them into court and questioned them. But even though they were faced with the highest religious authority, who had the power to exile them, Peter and John weren't intimidated. Acts 4:13 says that when the leaders "saw the courage of Peter and John and realized that they were unschooled, ordinary men, they were astonished and they took note that these men had been with Jesus." What a compliment to Peter and John that people could tell, simply by how they behaved, that they had been with Jesus. I want to live my life like that.

Even though our world is awfully loud right now, everyone saying this and claiming that, we tend to be pretty quiet about stuff that really matters. We can debate all day about celebrity news, politics, and entertainment, but we often stay quiet when we have the opportunity to share our faith. I'm not saying that every word you speak has to be about God. That wouldn't be authentic either.

But we can't be loud about the little stuff and silent about the most important thing in our lives.

But we can't be loud about the little stuff and silent about the most important thing in our lives.

Sometimes we hush up about our faith because we feel other people won't want to hear about it, that they will be offended, angry, or make fun of us. And maybe that will happen; you can't control how people respond. But in my experience, people are more curious about your experience with God than anything else. Humans are desperately hungry for anything that gives their lives meaning. And if you really believe that you have been saved by Christ, shouldn't you care enough about other people to risk talking to them about God?

I was talking to my sister recently about knowing when to talk about my faith with a friend, and she said, "Keep living your life, being a witness the way you are, and people will see the difference. Then they will make the adjustments in their life to be more in tune with the

Father." The most powerful way you can share your faith is by living it out in your actions. Seek to do everything you do with excellence so that in every conversation you have, in your work, through your studies, on the court, and in your relationships, people will recognize that you have a higher calling. "Whatever you do, work at it with all your heart, as working for the Lord," says Colossians 3:23.

So let your light shine. Don't be ashamed to speak boldly about your faith. God has called you to represent him to the world. Before he left his followers, Jesus gave them one last command to share his truth and love with others so that the people around them could know and follow him too. He promised, "And surely I am with you always, to the very end of the age" (Matthew 28:20).

WRITE

As you journal, consider what it means to live your faith out loud. Do you ever feel like you need to hide your faith? Have you ever felt too nervous to talk about your relationship with Christ in front of other people? Why did you feel this way? God has placed you in a specific place and time, and with specific people to be his light right where you are. How can you be an example of Christ to others where you live? How can you follow Jesus' last command with those around you? Write a prayer asking God to give you the guidance and confidence to represent him well, in every area of your life.

29

Wait on the Lord

"The LORD will fulfill his purpose for me; your steadfast love, O LORD, endures forever."

PSALM 138:8 (ESV)

Life comes at you fast. It seems like yesterday I was trying to get through high school, and now it has already been several years since I graduated college.

For some people, life takes off pretty smoothly after college. They graduate, land their dream job, marry their dream partner, buy the dream house, and their path to "making it" seems so easy. But it doesn't work like that for everyone. For a lot of us, our journeys seem to wander a little more, and every step along the way requires a little more time and patience. In high school, I thought I knew how my life would end up: I was going to do the whole college thing, play basketball, graduate, find my dream job, get married, travel the world with my wife, and then start a family. But I can tell you now that I only got the first few parts right.

Right after college, all my friends landed awesome jobs. Then soon they were all married. A few years later, those same friends began having kids and their careers were taking off. And while I kept working toward my goals, life just didn't cooperate the way I thought it would. I hadn't been at college for very long before my plans for a career in basketball were ruined. Then my dad was diagnosed with cancer. A transfer to a new college and a difficult breakup derailed my plans further. I felt like I had missed out on the magic ticket or something. Every time I checked social media, someone else was engaged or had received a promotion. I talked to one of my best friends about this and he asked, "What are we doing wrong?!"

A lot of young adults feel anxiety because they've been taught that a successful life happens in a specific order: college, job, marriage, family. And when their lives don't match that pattern, they believe their whole lives are ruined, that they'll never catch up. The biggest challenge is being patient and trusting God's reassurance that everything will be all right, even though sometimes, it sure doesn't feel that way.

In the Bible, God promised Abraham that he would be the father of many nations. But Abraham had to wait twenty-five years before Isaac was born. How many times do you think Abraham wondered if he had heard God correctly? But still, he had faith that God would keep his promises, and eventually God gave him Isaac. And then Isaac's son, Jacob, had twelve sons, and the descendants of those twelve became the tribes of Israel. Abraham must have felt frustrated during those long years of waiting, but God's timing was perfect. Many generations after Abraham, Jesus was born in the tribe of Judah, and he brought salvation to all nations. Abraham really did become the father of many nations; even you and I are his children through our faith in Jesus Christ.

The journey of my life has taken me all over the map. At times, it seemed it was taking me twice, even three times as long as my friends to get through college and hunt for a job, and figure out what my life is about. But looking back now, I can see God's timing was right on. I'm in a totally different place than where I thought I would be years ago, but I know this is exactly where God has called me to be. And I would never choose to be anywhere else. The fact that I'm writing this book right now is a testament that God's plans are better than ours. As Proverbs 19:21 tells us, "Many are the plans in the mind of a man, but it is the purpose of the LORD that will stand" (ESV).

We live in a fast-pasted society that runs on instant gratification. We want everything to happen right when we want it to happen, and that usually means now. But we have to remember that God's timing is perfect, even if it seems to take forever. God's plan for you might not include the typical schedule the world expects you to

But we have to remember that God's timing is perfect, even if it seems to take forever.

follow. So, don't panic if your life doesn't look like the lives of your friends or your siblings.

For all of you whose journeys have not followed the typical road map, I encourage you to stay patient and keep your head up. As hard as it may be at times, remember to wait on God. Be patient and trust in God's timing. You are following God, not the world; as a result, your life likely won't look like everyone else's. God has important things planned for you: "'For I know the plans I have for you,' declares the LORD, 'plans to prosper you and not to harm you, plans to give you hope and a future'" (Jeremiah 29:11).

REFLECT

Think about how long Abraham had to wait to see God's promise fulfilled. Can you relate to him in having to wait on God's timing? Does your life look like you thought it would? When you think about the future, what are you most anxious about? Are you willing to wait for God, even if that means waiting a few weeks, months, even years? As you think about this, pray and ask God to fulfill his purpose for your life. Ask him to give you the patience needed to wait for his perfect timing, and the peace to know that he's got it all in hand.

30

116

"God gave us a spirit not of fear but of power and love and self-control. Therefore do not be ashamed of the testimony about our Lord."

2 TIMOTHY 1:7-8 (ESV)

116: Music artist and rapper Lecrae has made these three numbers scream something important. He's rapped about them, worn them, and challenged so many to live the 116 life. The number 116 represents the verse in Romans 1:16: "For I am not ashamed of the gospel, because it is the power of God that brings salvation to everyone who believes."

As a college student, Lecrae became so passionate about this verse that he formed a group called 116 Clique with his friends Sho Baraka, Tedashii, and Trip Lee. At first, they were just a handful of students excited to share Jesus through music. Today, they are a group of award-winning artists. On their label website, they say, "Rather than find our significance in the status quo, we want to remember that success is not how well we've done compared to others, but how well we are doing what we were created to do." And for them, that means courageously rapping, singing, and living the good news of Jesus Christ.

Romans 1:16 is not just directed at Lecrae. God calls each one of us to spread the news that Jesus saves the lost. Each of us has a platform, a sphere of influence. Lecrae's platform is his music. People who listen to Lecrae are encouraged and challenged to press closer to God by his bold lyrics and honest songs. Although you might not be world-famous, you have a platform and more influence with your family, friends, community, and school than you realize. Don't waste it. Don't shy away from opportunities to speak out about your relationship with Christ.

Now, being bold to share our faith doesn't mean we need to wear T-shirts and make billboards that say, "Got Jesus?" We're not selling a product; we're talking about the living God. We all have that one friend who weaves their favorite topic into every conversation. But that's not always the best tactic to share God's love with others. Jesus teaches us to care more about the people we're with than the number of times we squeeze Scripture into the conversation. I want to make sure that the way I share my faith doesn't push people away from Jesus and

I want to make sure that the way I share my faith doesn't push people away from Jesus and instead helps them experience his life-changing love.

instead helps them experience his life-changing love. So what does that look like for you and me today?

I know how it is sometimes—that awkward moment when you have the chance to say something about God but you're not sure how your friends will react. What we need to keep in mind in those times is that we never know what God is doing behind the scenes in a person's life. We don't have to force our faith into every conversation, though when an opportunity arises, we need to be ready to speak up. 1 Peter 3:15 says, "Always be prepared to give an answer to everyone who asks you to give the reason for the hope that you have." I've been surprised when friends who seemed to have no interest in faith at all ask me about my relationship with Jesus. It's such an honor to be able to help them along their journey to finding God. Don't shrink away from these opportunities because of the fear of what they might think of you. So what if someone laughs, critiques my faith on social media, or argues with me. Jesus was beaten, spit on, humiliated, and crucified for me. This is the least I can do.

As you keep an eye out for opportunities to speak up, pray for those around you who do not know Jesus. Pray that God continues to work behind the scenes in their hearts and give them a hunger to know him.

It takes practice to learn how to speak out about our faith, and it may feel awkward at first. But remember that God is with you even then. He longs for everyone to know him and to experience his love. Let's make 116 a reminder to speak out when we have the opportunity to share our faith, living life unashamed.

REFLECT

Have you ever felt ashamed of being a Christian? What made you feel that way?

Just like the artists of 116 Clique have a musical platform to share their faith, God has given you a platform too. Reflect on all the people you live, work, and study with. What are the natural skills and the talents you've been given? How do you think God is calling you to use them to share his love with those around you?

As you reflect on how to live out your faith, pray for those in your life who don't know God. Ask God to give you the courage to be bold and to take every opportunity to share his love with them.

What Are You Waiting For?

You will be his witness to all people
of what you have seen and heard.
And now what are you waiting for?

ACTS 22:15-16

We've covered a lot of ground throughout this devotional journey. We've talked about faith in our day-to-day living, about spending regular time with God, and trusting him when it all just doesn't make sense. But before you close this book, I want to tell you a story about a young man who inspires me.

Samuel Kaboo Morris was a Liberian prince born in 1873. When Samuel was just fourteen years old, his people were attacked by an enemy tribe and he was kidnapped. He was held for ransom while his father, the chief, was forced to bring expensive gifts to his captors. But no matter what his father brought, it was never enough to free Samuel. Soon Samuel's tribe had nothing left to give, and as punishment, Samuel was beaten every day. Imagine what he must have felt like—he was once a prince, but now he was treated worse than a slave.

Then one day, Samuel saw a flash of light and heard a voice telling him to run. The ropes that bound him fell loose, and though his body was beaten, he suddenly had enough strength to escape. He wandered for two days in the jungle before he found his way to a coffee plantation. There, Samuel met Miss Knolls, a missionary who introduced him to the God that rescued him. Miss Knolls taught him about Paul's encounter with Jesus and Samuel became fascinated by the similarities in their stories. Having taught him all she knew, Miss Knolls encouraged Samuel to travel to America to learn from her pastor. Samuel dreamed about going to school and then returning to Liberia as a missionary to share God's love with his own people.

Samuel learned firsthand the change that happens when a person realizes that they are deeply loved by the creator of the universe. Even though Samuel had no money to travel, God guided him to a captain who needed another man on his crew. The story goes that by the time the ship arrived in America, the captain and most of the crew had become followers of Jesus because of Samuel's example.

Once arriving in New York, Samuel was met by Miss Knoll's pastor and lived in his home for a while. On his first night in America, Samuel led twenty people to Christ. He made such a difference for the people in that community that they raised funds to send Samuel to college to study theology. He arrived at Miss Knoll's alma mater, Taylor University, in 1891.

Samuel's authentic faith was magnetic. He was heard praying in his room long into the night. Frequently, students stopped by his dorm room to ask for advice and prayer. People from around the country traveled to hear him speak at the local churches. So many students who were unsure about their belief in God became passionate followers of Christ because of Samuel.

When you follow Jesus, your life isn't the only one that changes. If you live out your faith like Samuel, the lives of those around you will respond and change as well. There are many people all over the world today who have never heard about Jesus. Others have heard about him, but they have never seen someone

When you follow Jesus, your life isn't the only one that changes.

actually live out what the love of God looks like in a person's life. When people saw and talked with Samuel, they saw the reflection of Christ in his life and they heard about the love of God.

Samuel never saw his dream of returning home to share God's love and truth with his own people. After one year at college, he contracted pneumonia, and a few months later, he died. He was only twenty years old. The entire student body and hundreds of people from the surrounding area attended his memorial service. His death inspired several students to become missionaries in Africa to fulfill Samuel's dream. Samuel's legacy rippled across that small Midwest campus, then stretched all the way to Africa and around the world. And we are still seeing it today, as people like you and me learn what God can do with one individual completely committed to following him.

What's so inspiring to me about Samuel Kaboo Morris is that he didn't let anything hold him back from following God—not his age, not his lack of money and resources, not the language barrier. He kept his focus on Christ. How did he do that? We've talked a lot about the practical steps to following Christ. But it all boils down to seeking God with all your heart, your mind, and your soul. Like Samuel, I pray that each one of us will be so hungry to keep learning about Jesus that our passion will inspire others to discover God's love. I'm not there yet. Somedays I feel like I'm going backward, but I keep working hard toward the goal of thinking less about myself and more about God so that when others look at me, they see a reflection of Christ.

You are in a unique place to be a Samuel to your school, your team, your family, your friends. By seeking to know God closely, you can inspire those around you to do the same. You are God's child, his ambassador, his light to those around you. This is not some inspirational speech; this is fact. You represent the Hope that saves. And no matter what you have seen or done, and no matter what you will face in the future, you can trust that this is true: God is with you and he is for you. So what are you waiting for? Don't wait until you are older or when life makes more sense to put your faith in action. Because those around you can't wait. They need the hope that you have now.

It's only appropriate to leave you with a word from Paul, Samuel's spiritual brother and our faith model. What Paul writes here in Ephesians 3:16–18 is also my prayer for you as you continue following Christ. "I pray that out of his glorious riches he may strengthen you with power through his Spirit in your inner being, so that Christ may dwell in your hearts through faith. And I pray that you, being rooted and established in love, may have power, together with all the Lord's holy people, to grasp how wide and long and high and deep is the love of Christ."

You represent the Hope that saves.

REFLECT

As you read about Samuel's life, what challenges you? Samuel had no money, he wasn't famous, he had no support from family. Yet God used him in amazing ways to bring others to Christ. How do you think God is calling you to challenge, inspire, and encourage others to seek him?

Pray and thank God for his work around the world to give every one of his children a chance to know him. Ask for a hunger to keep learning about Jesus and to keep growing in your faith. And ask God to use your life, like Samuel's, to encourage others to draw closer to Jesus Christ.

Conclusion

Writing a book is not easy. There's a lot of hard work—a lot of phone call discussions, so many words, hours studying Scripture, and of course more revisions than I care to count. I realized that life doesn't slow down when you're writing a book. If anything, the writing of *A Higher Calling* came at one of the busiest seasons of my life. I married my beautiful wife, Jordin Sparks, and learned that we are expecting our first son! I also grieved the sudden death of two close friends. They are still missed today.

There were times when the writing was easy, fun, and creative. And there were times when I scrapped it all and began again. Life is like that sometimes. We scrap our original expectations and try again. But the process of writing each devotional gave me an opportunity to reflect and study the experience God has led me through. There were times of failing, times of learning, and times of growth. But each step, as wandering as it seemed, brought me closer to the holy, powerful God.

I hope that, as you've read this book, you've drawn a little closer to God as well. I hope you've been challenged, encouraged, comforted, and inspired to keep on.

In a way, growing your faith is like writing your own book. There are lots of questions, a lot of studying Scripture, and of course, lots of revisions. There will be times when your faith grows fast and strong, filling pages of lessons learned and favorite verses. And there will be times when the pages of your faith journey will fill painfully slow.

But this story that your faith is telling, it is yours alone to write. Nobody else will make sure that your faith journey is telling a good story. It's not the job of your parents, your pastor, or your youth leader to make sure that your relationship with God is healthy. Ideally, these people will help you fill in the pages, but your faith is not their responsibility. It is yours.

And we don't know how many pages we get to fill. Life is tragically short and the last page might be turned before we know it. So I encourage you to not sit back and coast. A relationship with God is too valuable to take lightly. Instead, keep going, keep learning.

Now that you've finished this book, find another study or devotional to read through. Pick a book of the Bible to read on your own. But keep pressing closer to God. I hope that you never stop growing, that all your life will be a process of finding your way closer to the living God. And I know that you will never have to go it alone. God is with you now, and he will be with you to guide and strengthen you through it all.

Acknowledgments

I want to acknowledge the love and support of my parents, Dana and Bridget; my siblings, Breanna and Blake; Gma and Papa Leo; Auntie Cynthia; my wife, Jordin; and the broskies, Tim, Leo, and Jermaine. Thanks also to Josh and Krista, the Wolfpack; 2 Live Crew; my college basketball coach, RJ "Roy" Barsh; and my college mentor, Ray Allen. A big thank you to Lecrae and Todd Dulaney, Shari Rigby, Annette Bourland, Estee Zandee, and the whole team at Zondervan.

Discussion Questions

1. How does it feel to realize that God calls you a son or daughter? You've been adopted into his holy family and he loves you unconditionally. What does this truth mean for how you live the rest of your life; what does it mean for how you live today?

    _____
    _____
    _____
    _____

2. Was there ever a time when you felt like your faith wasn't strong enough? Why is it hard to have faith in God? Discuss what it means for you to have faith that is "sure enough" God will work all things out in the end.

    _____
    _____
    _____
    _____

3. Are you a different person at church than at school or with your friends? Do you feel any disconnect between your faith and your daily life? Why do you

think that is? How can you grow toward being your authentic self no matter where you are?

_____

_____

_____

_____

_____

4. Just like we have role models we follow, we are often role models to someone else—our friends or siblings. Who is looking up to you? Talk about how you can be a better role model for them.

_____

_____

_____

_____

_____

5. When we're with friends, it can be hard to talk about Jesus or spiritual things. Why do you think that is? Share some ways you can encourage your friends to learn about God without making them feel pressured or uncomfortable.

_____

_____

_____

_____

_____

6. Sometimes our emotions or circumstances make it seem like God has left us, like he's not there

anymore. Have you ever felt this way? Is this feeling true? Discuss why you think we feel this way at times. What does God promise us?

_____

_____

_____

_____

_____

7. How comfortable are you with prayer? Does it ever feel hard to do, or does it make you nervous? Share why prayer may be difficult for you sometimes. If you prayed every day, how do you think it would change your relationship with God and with others?

_____

_____

_____

_____

_____

8. It is easier to speak than it is to listen, and this is true in our relationship with God too. When was the last time you tried to hear God speak to you? Discuss why it is so hard to listen to God's voice. Talk about ways that might help you listen to him.

_____

_____

_____

_____

_____

9. When you hear the word *obedience*, what comes to mind? What do you feel? Why do you think you feel that way? Think through what God's purpose might be in calling us to obey his commands. Does that change how you view obedience?

    _____

    _____

    _____

    _____

    _____

10. Has there ever been a time when you felt like you failed God somehow? What made you feel like that? How do you think God saw you in that moment? Talk through what God might be teaching you through that experience.

    _____

    _____

    _____

    _____

    _____

11. When was the last time you experienced God working in your life? What happened, and how did that affect your relationship with him?

    _____

    _____

    _____

    _____

    _____

12. Imagine for a moment that you never heard about Jesus. How would your life be different? What kind of a person do you think you would be? Discuss some of the changes you've seen in your life since you started following Jesus.

_____

_____

_____

_____

_____

13. When was the last time you talked about God with your friends? How did it go? If you could have that conversation over again, what would you do differently?

_____

_____

_____

_____

_____

14. If following Jesus means that your life doesn't get easier, but actually might get harder, why do it? Talk through what it means to follow God for the long haul, even if life doesn't turn out the way you hope it will.

_____

_____

_____

_____

_____

15. It's difficult to admit when we're wrong and when we need his forgiveness. When was the last time you asked God for forgiveness? Did you feel a difference after you talked to God? Discuss what it means to trust that, because of Jesus' death on the cross, God forgives you when you ask.

_____

_____

_____

_____

_____

16. Do you feel like you are moving closer to God, or farther away? Share the things that might be contributing to your direction right now. What do you hope your relationship with Jesus will be like in a month? What about in a year?

_____

_____

_____

_____

_____

17. Samuel Morris had a hunger to know more and more about God. What do you think is the next step for you to keep growing closer to God?

_____

_____

_____

_____

_____

Scripture Index

by devotion number

Connect with
Dana Isaiah Thomas!

 @_danaisaiah

 itsmeDanaIsaiah

 @_danaisaiah

A Higher Calling

Dana Isaiah Thomas

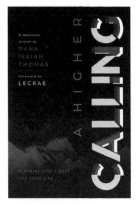

The ebook edition of *A Higher Calling: Claiming God's Best for Your Life* contains all the empowering and inspiring devotions in the print edition, but in a digital format that allows you to read a chapter or key passage from your phone, computer, or e-reading device wherever you are, whenever you need help letting go of fears and doubts or encouragement to draw closer to Christ.

In addition to the book content, **the ebook includes an exclusive workout and Scripture memorization plan** that helps you get your body and heart in shape.

Available in stores and online!

ZONDERVAN®
.com

Amanda Ramón

Dana I. Thomas was born in Chicago. He and his family moved to Missouri, where his parents took over a Christian camp summer ministry that specialized in sports and the gospel. He graduated from Southeastern University in Lakeland, Florida, where he truly developed his passion for writing devotionals. *A Higher Calling* is his first published work.